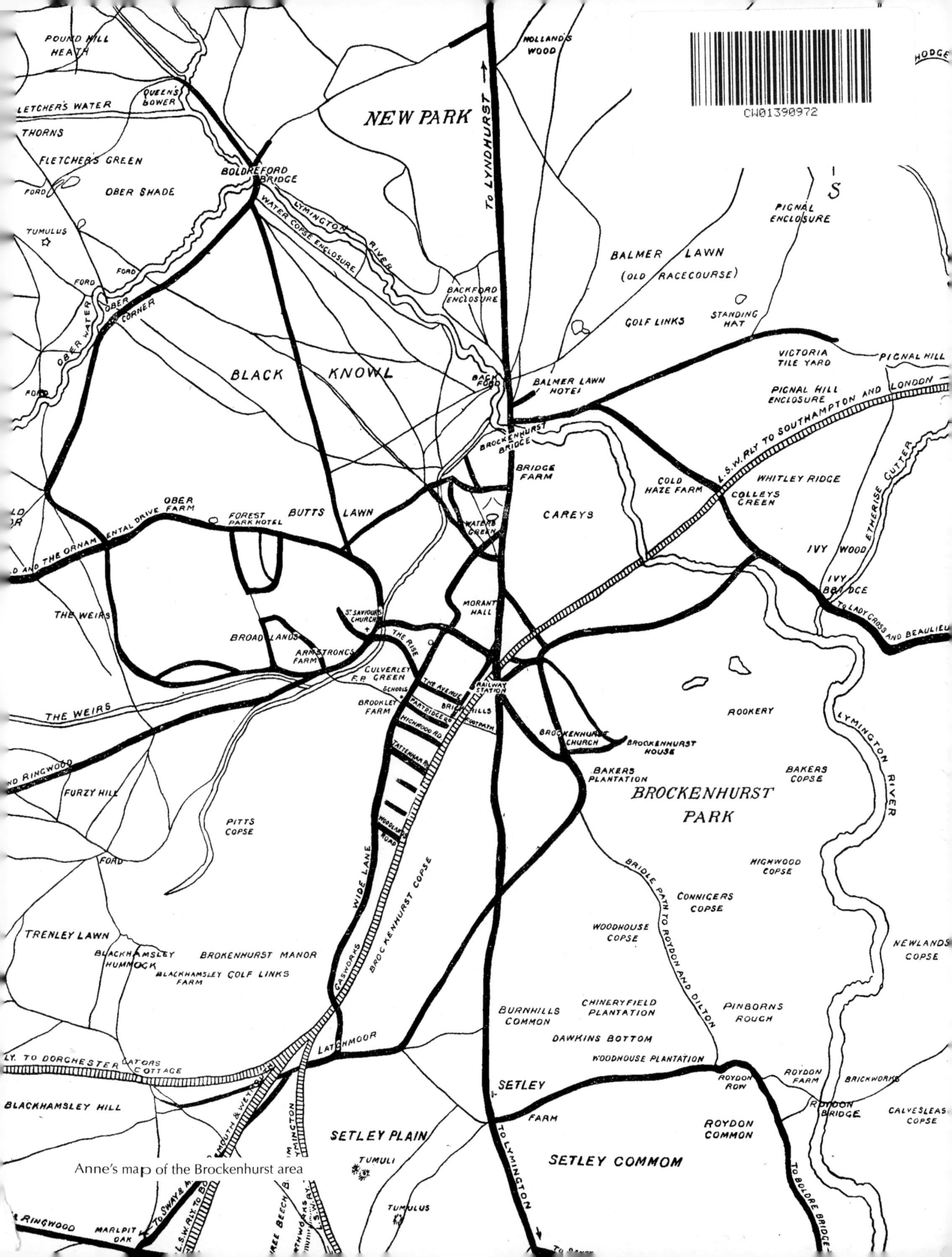

Anne's map of the Brockenhurst area

POUND HILL HEATH
HOLLAND'S WOOD
NEW PARK
FLETCHER'S WATER
QUEEN'S BOWER
THORNS
FLETCHERS GREEN
OBER SHADE
FORD
TUMULUS
FORD
FORD
OBER WATER
OBER CORNER
FORD
BOLDREFORD BRIDGE
WATER COPSE ENCLOSURE
LYMINGTON RIVER
TO LYNDHURST
BACKFORD ENCLOSURE
PIGNAL ENCLOSURE
BALMER LAWN (OLD RACECOURSE)
GOLF LINKS
STANDING HAT
VICTORIA TILE YARD
PIGNAL HILL
PIGNAL HILL ENCLOSURE
BLACK KNOWL
BACK FORD
BALMER LAWN HOTEL
BROCKENHURST BRIDGE
BRIDGE FARM
COLD HAZE FARM
COLLEYS GREEN
WHITLEY RIDGE
L.S.W. RLY TO SOUTHAMPTON AND LONDON
ETHERISE GUTTER
OBER FARM
FOREST PARK HOTEL
BUTTS LAWN
WATERS GREEN
CAREYS
IVY WOOD
IVY BRIDGE
TO LADY CROSS AND BEAULIEU
AND THE ORNAMENTAL DRIVE
THE WEIRS
BROAD LANDS
ST SAVIOUR'S CHURCH
THE RISE
ARMSTRONGS FARM
MORANT HALL
CULVERLEY F.P. GREEN
SCHOOLS
THE AVENUE
RAILWAY STATION
BROOKLEY FARM
BRIAR HILLS
FOOTPATH
PARTRIDGE RD
HIGHWOOD RD
TATTENHAM RD
BROCKENHURST CHURCH
BROCKENHURST HOUSE
ROOKERY
LYMINGTON RIVER
THE WEIRS
RINGWOOD
FURZY HILL
PITTS COPSE
FORD
WIDE LANE
WOODLANDS ROAD
BROCKENHURST COPSE
BAKERS PLANTATION
BROCKENHURST PARK
BAKERS COPSE
HIGHWOOD COPSE
CONNIGERS COPSE
BRIDLE PATH TO ROYDON AND DILTON
TRENLEY LAWN
BLACKHAMSLEY HUMMOCK
BROKENHURST MANOR
BLACKHAMSLEY GOLF LINKS FARM
GASWORKS
WOODHOUSE COPSE
NEWLANDS COPSE
BURNHILLS COMMON
CHINERYFIELD PLANTATION
PINBORNS ROUGH
DAWKINS BOTTOM
WOODHOUSE PLANTATION
LY. TO DORCHESTER
GATORS COTTAGE
LATCHMOOR
SETLEY
FARM
ROYDON ROW
ROYDON FARM
BRICKWORKS
BLACKHAMSLEY HILL
SOUTH & WEST
LYMINGTON
TO LYMINGTON
SETLEY COMMOM
ROYDON COMMON
ROYDON BRIDGE
CALVESLEAS COPSE
SETLEY PLAIN
TUMULI
TUMULUS
RINGWOOD
MARLPIT OAK
L.S.W. RLY TO BO
TO SWAY & R
FREE BEECH B
PORTSMOUTH & W
TO BANK
TO BOLDORE BRIDGE

Anne McEntegart: *The Bull*, woodcut, 1920s, courtesy of Dumfries Museum.

Contents

Presented by:
Emma Robson, Martin Edwards
RMC Books – (0114) 250 6300

Design by:
Paul Cocker
RMC Books – (0114) 250 6300

Contributors:
Chris Brierley, Ann Beedham

First Published in 2011 on behalf of:
The Trustee of the Estate of Anne McEntegart

Published by:
RMC Books
Broadfield Court
Broadfield Business Park
Sheffield S8 0XF
(0114) 250 6300
www.rmcbooks.co.uk

Wild ponies graze freely in the New Forest

Anne and Mac with their son John in 1934.

Foreword

Postcard of Bolderwood Bridge and Queen's Bower in the late 1930s. Courtesy of Tony Johnson.

A cruel effect of war is the way it scatters families. At the start of World War II, in 1939, artist Anne McEntegart faced a horrible choice. Her husband, Group Captain Bernard McEntegart, believed that a Nazi invasion was very likely and wanted their only child, seven year old John, to go to relatives in Newfoundland. Agonisingly, Anne had to decide whether to go too, or whether to remain with Bernard. She stayed with her husband in London.

Then, in 1943 Bernard was posted abroad. Now alone and wishing to expand her role in the war effort, Anne decided to leave the capital. She volunteered to work full-time on a farm in the New Forest. New Park Farm, run by Walter Gossling, was just outside the village of Brockenhurst (population in 1931: 2,482). It was most probably suggested by Anne's older sister, Vera who was lodging in Brockenhurst to be close to her husband. He was working in Beaulieu with the Special Operations Executive, training secret agents to carry out sabotage and subversion behind enemy lines. Unfortunately, less than a month after Anne arrived, Vera went back home to Edinburgh.

Beecham Wood, Brockenhurst circa 1910.

At thirty-eight, Anne was much older than the land girls at New Park. But she did exactly the same work. Though she was, in fact, just within the age limit for membership of the Women's Land Army, she did not apply to join, probably because she wanted to be free to leave if her husband came home. The members of the W.L.A., who were usually unmarried, signed on until the war ended, whenever that might be.

From her first day on the farm, June 29 1943, Anne kept a diary. She had found lodgings in a house in the village, "Holbrook House", which is still there today. It was in her quiet top floor room that Anne must have written the diary. It was a way of talking with herself her about new life; one that was taken up with milking cows, delivering milk by horse and cart, weeding, harvesting and ploughing. All around her she was aware of more and more preparations being made for the Normandy Landings, for D-Day. How she found the time and energy to write her diary is a matter of wonder. Anne had no time to paint, but in the diary she painted with words. Her writing vividly pictures her experiences.

She gradually came to enjoy the New Forest countryside. Once, after a brief "holiday" back in London, she describes how she felt happy returning to New Park Farm. Cycling to work that morning, "everything looked beautiful in the golden morning sunlight, with a blue sky. The old farmstead looked peaceful and serene and continuing. I felt proud that I was part of it..."

What she was "part of" was a small community of workers and milk customers; conceivably a kind of temporary family. Although she enjoyed her own company, Anne's diary celebrates more than anything else the people she was working with.

Not to mention a certain pony...

War Events Timeline:
National and International Events

1943:

May 16:	RAF Dambusters Operation
July 10:	Allied invasion of Sicily
July 25:	Mussolini overthrown
August 17:	Sicily in Allied hands
September 3:	Allies (including Eighth Army) invaded Italian mainland
September 7:	Italy surrendered. German Army – in strength – siezed Rome
October 1:	Naples captured by Allies
November 6:	Kiev taken by Russians
November 28:	Churchill, Roosevelt and Stalin met in Tehran
December 2 :	UK – men directed to coal mines "The Bevin Boys"
December 26:	German battleship Scharnhorst sunk

1944:

June 4:	Rome captured by Allies. King of Italy abdicated
June 6:	D-Day invasion of Europe (over 4,000 ships)
July 20:	"Bomb plot" attempt on Hitler's life
August 1:	Warsaw uprising
August 25:	Paris liberated
September 3:	Allies entered Belgium
September 8:	First V-2 fell on England
September 11:	Allied forces in German territory
October 3:	Warsaw rising crushed by German troops
December 16:	German counter-offensive in the Ardennes

1945:

January 17:	Russians captured Warsaw
February 14:	Dresden bombed
March 6:	Cologne captured by Allies
April 11:	Russians entered Vienna after seven-day battle
April 28:	Mussolini and mistress shot by Italian partisans
April 30:	Hitler killed himself and mistress
May 2:	Germans in Italy surrendered. Berlin captured by Russians
May 8:	End of Second World War against Germany. VE Day celebrated
June 26:	United Nations Charter signed at San Francisco
July 26:	British General Election. Huge Labour majority – Churchill succeeded by Clement Attlee as Prime Minister
August 6:	Atomic bomb on Hiroshima
August 9:	Nagasaki – second atomic bomb
August 14:	Japan surrendered unconditionally to Allies

(Reproduced in part from *Before We Go: Brockenhurst Memories of Peace and War c.1914-1945* by Richard Taylor, MBE 1995)

The dense foliage of the New Forest is a haven for wildlife

Telephone 3127 Brockenhurst.

W. H. GOSSLING,

NEW PARK FARM DAIRY, BROCKENHURST.

WINNER OF NUMEROUS PRIZES.   ALL MILK SOLD PRODUCED BY MY OWN COWS.

June 16/43

Dear Mr Entejast.

I have enclosed a letter to the Ministry of Labour as requested.

I hope that when you are here you will find both your work and general surroundings agreeable.

Yours faithfully
W. H. Gossling

This genial letter from Walter Gossling, the New Forest farmer who was to be Anne's boss, certainly made her welcome. The land girls, including Walter's daughter Dorothy, not to mention his wife, would take time to warm to the newcomer.

The Milk Lady at New Park Farm

The Wartime Diary of Anne McEntegart
June 1943-February 1945

Tuesday June 29th 1943

My First Day At New Park Farm[2]

I wakened at quarter to four, to see a red dawn lighting the sky and three hours later, when I was cycling along the narrow bumpy track to my work across the Moor, the sun was already bright and warm and the air like ice – a glorious morning. And what a wonderful ride across the dew-laden moor then into the dark, still forest and along the wide cart track to the farm.

GIANT BEECHES NEW FOREST

WHERE I ENTER THE FOREST EVERY MORNING

Anne's diary of her time at New Park Farm was handwritten in two notebooks. This is the cover of the first book. She cycled to work early every day in all weathers from her lodgings, Holbrook House, in Brockenhurst.
The illustration shows her daily route.

I was sent to watch "Freda"[3] in the Dairy – a trim, efficient little girl with brown arms and a brown, fresh face, dressed in the khaki dungarees and green jersey of the Land Army. She was carefully preparing the milk cooler for the new milk which was already being brought in by the men. This we poured in at the top and it came seeping through in tiny trickles and down into the churn. Freda then got busy filling the bottles and placing them in iron carriers for the "Round". There are two rounds; Freda takes one and Eileen takes the other.

Soon Eileen[4] arrived "late as usual" and asked me to watch her harness the pony, as I was to go with her. We went into the paddock and caught Peter, harnessed him into the float and set off.

Eileen is a tall, blonde, very attractive, provocative creature – with a retroussé nose and a ridiculously small red mouth. She has very long, agile, colt-like legs, dressed in tight, washed-out blue dungarees. Above this, she wears a highly embroidered woolly jacket, gay Swiss gloves, and her back hair hung in a net with coloured spots dangling all over it. She really looked a Queen Boadicea in this little chariot with her carefree abandonment and her sulky mien which I soon saw was her chief method of attack.

The initial coolness on the farm towards Anne – perhaps because she was the well-spoken, well-educated wife of a Royal Air Force officer – soon melted away. At thirty-eight, she was also quite a lot older than the other girls. Perhaps this is why she is content to remain in the background in this photo. From left to right are Dorothy Gossling, the farmer's daughter; Eileen (surname unknown); Barbara Carter; Anne; and Freda Sque.

My memory of the "Round" is a haze of hundreds of houses with jugs or bottles outside their doors, up little lanes, along winding avenues, over corners of moor and even across streams and where we went I know not, but in and out we rushed with cans of milk, filling jugs or leaving bottles and always at my back was Eileen saying "A pint and a ½ here, one 'free' or 2 'cheap'" and warnings such as "No milk without money here." "Get out quick before they can ask for more." "She's awful." "Another house where they think money can buy everything!"

And so we went on and on for 5 solid hours. The sun shone and the wind blew and the little pony trotted gaily away, shaking the tassels on his ear caps to ward off the following flies, and all the way, Eileen gave me the "low-down" on every house we reached till my mind was in a whirl and only a few incidents stand out clearly – like our arrival at the General's Headquarters (Royal Marines) in a lovely country house[5] where we walked into the kitchen "for our morning coffee" which is apparently always served, together with long, crisp rashers of bacon, still in the frying pan for the General's breakfast! Quarter of an hour's back chat with the marines, then a tour of the stables to see the General's new hunters and then on again with much shouting from the rear and "see you tomorrow"! (I gather we leave ½ a pint extra here to make up for our coffee!).

Then an inspection of a rabbit hutch to see "the babies" – four of them, all different colours. A house with a great mongrel who barred my way and snapped at my legs. "Don't mind him" shouted Eileen, "his bark's really worse than his bite!" The kind old dame, totally deaf, who brought us each out a glass of orange squash, and all the many old dames who wanted extra milk because they had visitors who had either been blitzed or were too young or too aged to digest anything but milk! How difficult that was for they could not understand that we were "short" and only went into a lengthy dissertation on how they were Mr Gossling's oldest customers!

We left for the "Round" at 8.30 and got back at 2.30. Then we had lunch (our packed lunch which we had brought with us) in the farm kitchen. The others had finished, so we had a peaceable meal with a great bowl of raspberries "to finish up" left by the family. Then came the milking. I milked two cows, Daisy and General, not too unsuccessfully, but my arms ached terrifically and Joe, the cowman, finished them off for me.

Afterwards, I helped Freda to wash out the milk bottles and then I swept out 2 cow byres. How heavy that great brush was! Exhausted, I rode home at 5 o'clock and lay flat on my bed, worn out!

MILKING - RIGHT POSITION   **MILKING - WRONG POSITION**

How to milk a cow in one easy lesson. At least, that was the intention of this illustration from *A Book of Farmcraft*, 1942 by Michael Greenhill. Evelyn Dunbar, an official war artist did all the illustrations for *A Book of Farmcraft*, which was aimed at farm workers, often townspeople, whom wartime farms had to increasingly rely on. This book, in its practical clarity, comes very close to Anne's attitude to farming. She puts it this way in the Diary: "I like the FUNCTIONAL-NESS of farming – it is so 'big' and all done for a purpose. There is nothing finicky or pernickety about it." Because Dunbar's drawings and Anne's diary are so much in tune, the diary is appreciatively peppered with the drawings from *A Book of Farmcraft*.

Wednesday June 30th

My Second Day

Cycled this morning over a dark, gloomy moor with rain clouds darkening the sky. I wore thick clothes and felt the cold air exhilarating on my face.

I milked "Topsy," a nice, easy cow, and found my arms less aching than yesterday. Then off on the Round Eileen and I went.

Bray, the lovely red setter, followed us and we were afraid of dog fights, so when we got to the gate at the foot of the "mess" drive, we decided to try and shut him out and hope he would go home. I held Bray while Eileen shut the gate. Peter the pony heard the click of the gate and dashed away up the hill. Bray cleared the gate in one leap and together they raced along, pulling up in front of the mess kitchen quite unattended. What amusement there was! The kitchen staff rushed to the top of the hill and jeered when they saw us miles below. "Eileen! Anne! Where are you?" they shouted.

Morant Hall, Brockenhurst, was built by the local "Lords of the Manor" in 1911 as a community centre for the whole area. It boasted a dance hall, a stage, a supper room, and, at the back, squash and tennis courts. Stars of the tennis circuit warmed up here before heading for Wimbledon. Frequent dances took place at the Hall as some locals still remember, and more than a few marriages sprang from first encounters here. Morant Hall, by then beyond repair, was demolished in 1971-2.

In August 1926 Anne set off with her older sister Vera on a trip round Germany. Anne's sketchbook from the time has survived. It is packed with charm and astute observations – such as this lively dog, not at all concerned to pose for the artist.

We had our usual coffee and chatter and complicated plans were made for a dance at the Morant Hall for tonight. "You must come Anne" said Chopper, a hairdresser in civil life. "Oh! I'm too old" I said. "Rubbish – you're in your prime and Jock here doesn't dance and I don't want to dance all the time". Jock, the nice fat Scots chef from Perthshire, smiled encouragingly and once more we hopped into our float and trotted away. It is a bit tricky being matey and knowing just how to draw the line somewhere!

One house I went to a dog sprang at me and snapped. "Will he bite?" I asked. "Oh, not much" replied a smiling mistress. "Remember his name's Pepper and if you say to him 'Pepper I'll have your bone' he won't bite you – he'll run after his bone instead!" I hope I shall remember which is Pepper out of all the numbers of dogs who spring at my legs and growl!

After dinner, I milked 3 cows and each was more successful than the last. Then I helped wash milk bottles, sweep out the byres and came home (5pm). My body is aching from head to foot. But I feel reassured in my mind, so physical fatigue is pleasant.

July 1st

My 3rd Day

A wonderful hot, sunny July day. Glorious to be on the float with the sun pouring down and a little breeze which we made as we trotted along. But jolly hot lugging the 2½ gallon pail to 125 houses, often down long drives and always "round to the back door". Every gate has a different latch and they all must be securely fastened to prevent the forest ponies from walking into the gardens. It is a long round, and running to the doors it takes a solid six hours. We leave at 8.30 and get back at 2.30 (for our dinner!) very hungry.

Peter the pony was tormented by flies and 3 times he bolted – once in the village street when we were in a house, an invalid shouted that he could see him from his window turn round and rush towards home. We caught him, but later when we were far up on the weirs (the high moorland) we returned from a little circle of houses to find no Peter and no float! In all the heat we trudged for quite ½ mile with the can between us and a large box of eggs. There we found Peter, almost hidden by bracken, turned down a hillside with the float tipped all up on one side and the reins twisted round and round the pony's front legs. However, how he and the float failed to roll over at such an angle I just do not know. The boss says we'll have to tie him up, but that will take so long – to tie him and untie him 125 times!

Joe Fripp, head cowman at New Park. He appears frequently throughout the diary – a man of teasing wit, character, wisdom and mood changes not helped by a big appetite. Anne obviously liked writing about him. She almost always refers to him as "old Joe," a matter of regard rather than a comment on his age – he was only in his forties.

After the hot sunshine, it was really very pleasant to go into the cool cowshed and take a hand at the milking. Rows of cows (we are milking 48) in their stalls chewing the cud peacefully and 4 or 5 milkers busy, so that the only sound is the pss pss, in higher and low pitched tones of milk swishing into pails and old Joe the Cowman[6] softly crooning "There's a Silver Lining", "A Little Grey Home in the West" and "John Peel" – his repertoire which is repeated day after day!

I milked "Peggy", "Daisy", "Topsy" and "General" and stripped General most successfully. At the snappy dog house, I said with great determination: "Pepper, I'll have your bone" and sure enough he turned tail and went into the kitchen to guard his bone! It was like a witch's spell to see the metamorphosis!

July 2nd

A peaceful scene of daily life in a country at war. This photo of Anne on one of the farm's milk floats, with her favourite pony Peter in the harness, shows how she had clearly adapted to her new role. Freda, years later, described the milk round: "Two women... delivered the milk to two-hundred and fifty customers. Bottles were used at first, but as the war went on glass broke and wasn't replaced... customers would place their jugs on the step" to be filled by the milk ladies from the large steel containers carried on their milk floats.

My Fourth Day

Entering the dark forest in the grey of early morning, I suddenly saw 2 specs of vivid, iridescent blue on the green bank – two kingfishers who flew far down the river as I approached; a lovely splash of colour along the dark brown of the muddy stream.

Instead of early milking, I caught Peter, groomed and harnessed him and prepared the float for the milk round. We take six carriers which hold 12 or 16 bottles each, a large churn with brass bindings and a tap, holding 15 gallons, a smaller churn of 10 gallons and a 2½ gallon can for carrying to each house. Quite a load. Every container must be tied securely because of jolting and on certain days, eggs and dried eggs must be taken. On Saturdays, the books are paid.

This was a broiling hot day – a real scorcher – and it was difficult to hurry. We got back rather late and milking took longer than usual as this is "weighing day" when each cow's milk is weighed and a record kept on a big chart.

July 3rd

My Fifth Day

I gaily volunteered to catch Peter, who was turned out with Danny in the big meadow. But I soon found it was easier said than done. Peter refused to be caught. The minute I went near him, he lay flat his ears, swung round on his heels and was off – likewise Danny!

Eileen came to help with a can of oats, but we couldn't get near him. Then Freda came too and we three tried to corner him, but quite unsuccessfully. We knew it was hopeless and the Boss knew too,[7] but he just left us there for about half an hour. When finally he did come, Peter walked up to him, stood still to be stroked and walked calmly with him to the stable! The Boss says Peter is a woman-hater!

Of course, we started off late and it was all a great rush as Eileen is going away on leave and wanted to be home early. How we dashed around in the heat of a "flaming July" day – but we made it. Eileen got away and I am to do the Round by myself tomorrow!

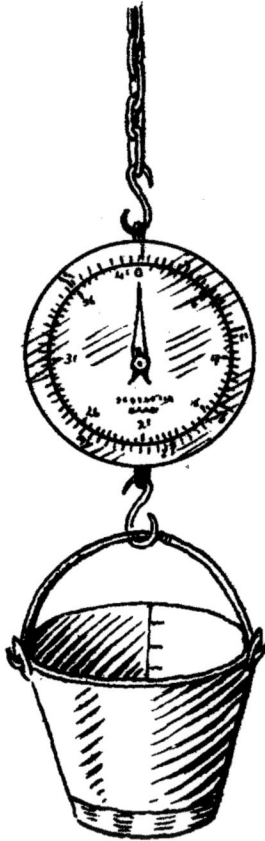

MILK WEIGHING MACHINE

(Evelyn Dunbar illustration).

Anne had known about horses since childhood and so was familiar with details like this, set out for the benefit of those unfamiliar with rural life. Peter received her energetic grooming attentions, and according to her sister Vera, looked a great deal better for the pampering.

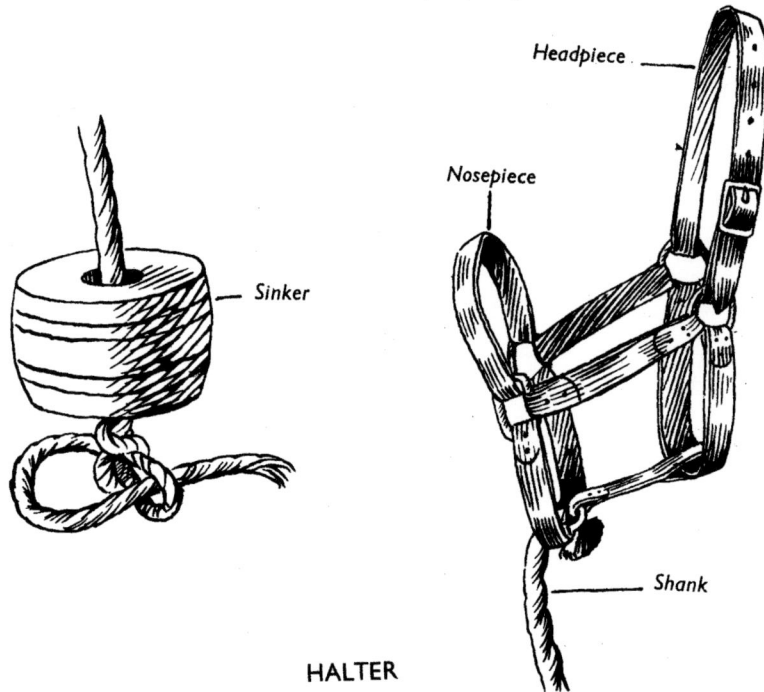

Headpiece

Nosepiece

Sinker

Shank

HALTER

Curry-Comb

Dandy-Brush

Body-Brush

E.D.

GROOMING TOOLS

July 4th – Sunday

My Sixth Day

I took some of my precious tea-party lump sugar to tempt Peter today but he was in the paddock and not too difficult to catch. I gave him a good grooming, harnessed him, loaded up the float and got off in good time.

I felt rather nerve wracked and very slow, but I did the round with no mistakes. And, although I felt exhausted, I was well satisfied with myself. Six days ago it was all complete confusion to me.

July 5th – Monday

My Seventh Day – A Day of Great Disaster

Determined to be nice and quick today, I set off gaily and trotting along at a good speed I suddenly heard the most awful crash and, looking around, I saw my 15 gallons milk churn lying on the road with 15 gallons of milk pouring in a frothy stream! The rope had snapped! I suppose the old rope had been there for donkey's years and it really wasn't my fault, but I felt sick with horror and stumbled blindly onwards to the General's Headquarters. The men were so kind. They said it was a perfect disgrace I should be sent out with a contraption like that and Chopper insisted on making me a cup of hot coffee himself and when I demurred, he said "Now Anne – if you don't have something you'll be tired and nervy and wretched, so you've just got to have it". I am eternally grateful to him and to them all. They just gave me the necessary courage to go on.

I had only ½ of my 10 gallon churn left and about 80 bottles, so I decided to cut everybody down to ½ a pint (except children and invalids) and see how far I could get round. Everyone was most kind, but it was dreadful repeating this dismal story again and again at each house to explain matters and it was obvious that they thought it was my fault because I was new. Mercifully, I just got round to every house and had a little over to make up a few extras. Then I had to take Peter to be shod at the Smithy, then home and lunch at 4pm!

Mr Gossling was out and I wonder what he will say tomorrow. The girls were ripping and full of sympathy. They all agreed it was jolly bad luck on my second day and that it was not my fault.

A dear old housekeeper, wearing a white mob cap, said she'd heard I came from Eton Square and so she'd let me out of the front door. Through the kitchen I was led and across a polished parquet hall in my heavy boots with my milk pail and out of the front door!

When I heard on the 9 o'clock news that General Sikorski and all his staff had been killed,[8] I was able to get my own disaster more in its proper proportion.

July 6th – Tuesday

My Eighth Day

The Boss was very friendly and kind about yesterday's disaster. He said it was just an accident and proceeded to recount more, much worse accidents – how the whole float-full of milk had been overturned – 60 gallons in one go! etc., so I felt reassured and ready for the fray once more.

Nothing of great import happened on this round, except that I got caught in a terrific thunderstorm, with rain beating down in sheets, thunder cracking overhead and flashes of lightening across the sky. Peter didn't mind a bit and we trotted along the high road which was swimming with water. It was exhilarating and exciting and although I was soaked to the skin, I didn't seem to mind – so unlike getting wet in town, where you become just bedraggled and miserable.

As I had set out on a lovely summer morning, I had nothing to change into except cycling leggings, which failed to cover my nakedness. "Auntie" pulled her large blue frock from over her head saying "It's time I had a fresh one anyway" (it was!) and handed it to me. It was simply immense and wound round me exactly three times. And David thought I was his mummy! Mr Gossling roared with laughter when he saw me crossing the farmyard and he has been amused ever since.

When unharnessing Peter, I found the harness almost in bits. Three vital parts were already tied with bits of string and today the fourth vital part just fell apart. His other harness has been at the menders for over a year and they refuse to mend anything except the Italian Prisoners of War shoes![9] I suppose I shall go on using this till there is another "accident" – I can see how philosophical a farmer is. He accepts the good with the bad and the frightful losses he has are just part of his scheme of things. His whole crop may be ruined in a night, any "accident" may occur at any moment, like Gabriel Oak in Hardy's "Far from the Madding Crowd,"[10] ruin may face him again and again and still he goes on calmly and stoically. It is a wonderful way to face life.

Anne's drawing of a two-day old calf suckling, taken from her German trip sketchbook, 1926.

Wednesday July 7th

An uneventful, very pleasant day. Fresh and cool after the storm and everyone feeling revived – I sprang from house to house till midday when it got really hot again and, as usual, I was a bit late getting home and had my lunch at 4pm.

We tried to feed a new calf who refused to suck – what a job it was. We were all covered in milk and he sneezed milk all over my face. He got the idea just at the end, so we hope tomorrow will be easier.

Thursday July 8th

A very good day – I got off early in the morning – decided to whip Peter up and get him "moving." We fairly sped and I actually got back before Freda. As I was turning into New Park drive, I happened to turn round and saw her behind so we both whipped up our ponies and raced down the avenue beneath the ancient oaks, and I won! Yesterday I told Mr Gossling I was too "old" to be quick, so today he smiled and said "A bit younger today, what?"!

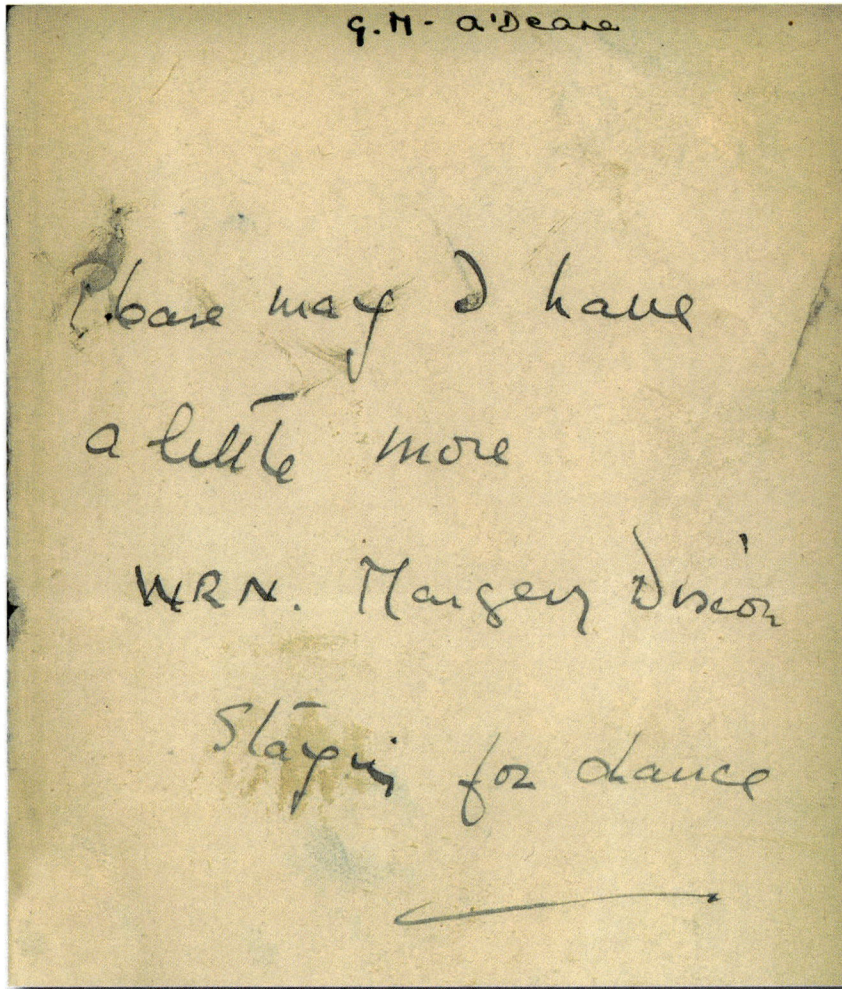

It is a measure of Anne's fascination with the smallest details of her work at the farm that she kept a number of the notes her milk round customers left on their doorsteps. Most of them were polite. Sometimes there were complaints, though not always true, that milk had gone sour – a reminder that there were few refrigerators.

Friday July 9th

A day of rain but I enjoyed it. It was so wild and exciting, especially up on the weirs, with a wind blowing across the moor and the rain beating in my face. Peter was gay and alive too and cantered along in grand style. Everyone who opened their doors shivered and said "What a miserable day – and so cold", but I was glowing with warmth and I enjoyed it. Milked 3 cows.

Saturday July 10th

Another pelting wet day. I got soaked to the skin but felt very happy – it is a grand life, using every muscle to the last inch and being so busy there is just not a minute to think. This was payday and it was a lengthy procedure. None remembered till they saw me. Then there was a hunt for their purse, then of course I had to add it all up while they chattered ceaselessly and then of course they had no small money, but it was interesting and I just resigned myself to being late. I got back at 4pm for my lunch. I can't help feeling pleased when so many people say "How brave you are" and "You are doing your bit."

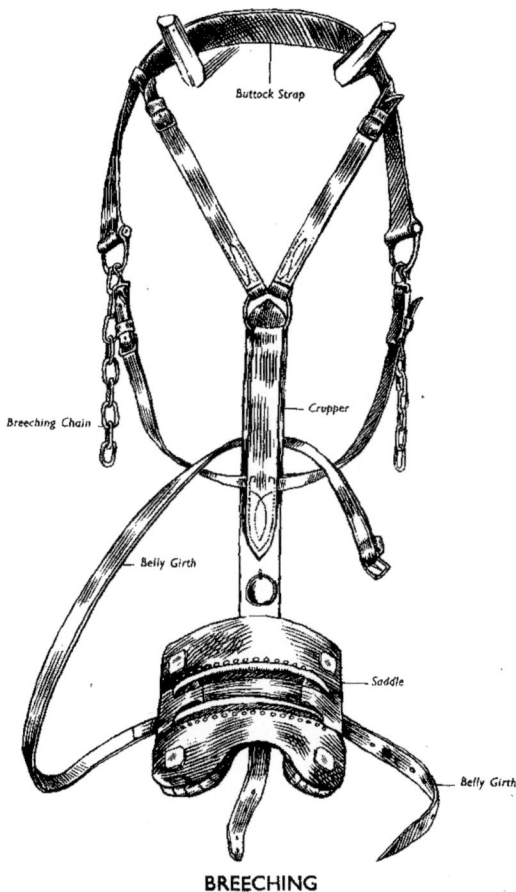

BREECHING

The "breeching" goes round the horse's buttocks and enables him, when between the shafts of a cart, to stop a moving load, to break it going downhill, or to push it backwards. (Evelyn Dunbar illustration).

Sunday July 11th

Another piece of my harness fell to bits just as I was setting off. Luckily I hadn't got far. It was the girth strap under Peter's tummy and old Joe tied it up with a bit of thin twine, which I suppose will have to last for the rest of time. Yesterday, Freda's shaft broke right off and she had to come back and get a big float which, when she came home, the boys said its wheels were almost off! Nobody takes the least interest and Mr Gossling doesn't even bother to look!

A nice peaceful day being Sunday, with balmy air and a nice breeze blowing. The scents of the gardens were intoxicating after the rain. I can hardly believe the gardens are true. They are like story book gardens after London and I stare at them and wonder if they can be real. The roses this year are magnificent, especially the ramblers which hang everywhere in great profusion. All the little cottage gardens which are entirely untended are a riot of scent and colour, with all the glowing flowers I had almost forgotten – phlox, sweet williams, honeysuckle, pinks and lavender, etc.

July 16th Friday

Back to work again after 2 days "off." How blissful it was to relax and potter about and do everything in slow time. I loved it, but I felt so well and so full of energy that I was up at 7am and didn't want to rest. That shows how fit I must be. I feel better and more vigorous than I have felt for years. And I was actually pleased to be back on the farm again and did my round in record time. I was pleased also to hear that Mr Gossling said it was a long time to go without a break at the beginning and he thought it was "wonderful". And they all said how they'd missed me!

It was glorious to be driving Peter again and a lovely day. We had some fine canters and although Mr Gossling said he thought the bottom of the float might drop out, but might "do a turn or two more," nothing untoward happened. I rode Peter bareback down to the big meadow and then milked four cows. Another grand day of really hard work and lovely sunshine.

Vera[11] and the soldiers say Peter looks quite different since I've been grooming him. A little boy had ranged 8 jam jars of every size and shape in a long line across the doorstep for me to fill with milk.

Saturday July 17

A very hot and rather hectic day. Jack Phillips[12], the old cowman, was ill, so I had to go away to the long meadow and catch Peter (a job the men usually do when he is out there), then I had to rearrange my float and load up the opposite way about so that the weight of my big churn would not coincide with a loose plank. This all made me late setting off and the heat and a sore foot didn't help me to hurry. Also, it was payday again and I got later and later and the climax was reached on my return to the village when I was besieged at every corner by people who said their milk was sour and would I give them more. They had had it from last night's churn and it was thundery in the night. Dear me! I had to cajole them and when, at last, I landed home, simply dying for a sit down and a bit of lunch at 4.15pm, Joyce[13] shouted from the cowshed that they were relying on me to help them out with the milking. They were short without Phillips and the other men were out in the hay fields. So I swallowed a sandwich and got into the job, but feel very exhausted tonight.

Sunday July 18th

A day of grumbles. Lots of milk had gone sour. Angry old women stood in the Beaulieu Road waving their jugs at me and made all sorts of complaints. Some had phoned the farm yesterday and Mr Gossling had told one it was the weather, another that the milk had been put into a dirty churn and a third that one must have been put into a dirty jug. This poor old dame was literally weeping tears of indignation – "Never, never in all her life had she been so insulted" and I felt sorry for her because her house is simply shining with elbow grease.

Jock, the cook at Whitley Ridge, lived in Basil Street mansions for 8 years as chef, so we had a good chatter about London in general and Knightsbridge in particular. He is one of the best and they are all so nice and never fail to have a can of steaming coffee waiting for me and a cheery call as I arrive at the top of the long drive. "Hulloa Anne!".

I got back in good time and milked two more difficult cows. Quite a promotion. I want to be able to milk them all, even the "kickers", whose hind legs have to be tied.

Monday July 19

Rather a beastly day, where I set off late, through no fault of my own, and lost time all the way along. It is the old "Court Martial Story" – it doesn't matter what good reasons you have, you are just late and that is all! It rained all day from 6am when I got up till 9.30pm when I am writing this. I got water logged and dispirited – especially when Chopper said it would take a good 4 or 5 years to finish this "show." I thought of doing the milk round for another 4 and nearly expired! Old Mrs Gulliver said if her milk turned sour again, she'd summons me for delivering it, as well as Mr Gossling for providing it.

I have strained my ankle and it is very sore and very tiring. Not a good day.

Tuesday July 20

My humour was restored today and the sun shone and I had an amusing occurrence which made me laugh. Some men had a rubber water pipe across the road with water pouring through. Thinking that Peter would probably jib, I was just stopping him to get out and lead him across when he suddenly swung round on his heels and backed the cart into a ditch which was already 3 or 4 feet deep in flowing water (from the pipe). I was flung into the ditch, luckily feet first, and as I scrambled out of the water, men got hold of Peter and stopped further mishap. I was most amused because people came rushing out of their cottages with red, excited faces and I looked in such a plight and yet I seemed to bounce off like a piece of India rubber and wasn't hurt a bit.

After the milking, we were told to take the cows up to the "Queen's Meadow" where they must go for a week or so for richer grass. Joyce and I and the two boys went and it was so lovely. We take them right through one of the most beautiful spots in the forest, past "Queen's Bower" and along a track right under the giant beeches. Several people are needed to herd them as they wander away into the open forest. It was a glorious sight to watch these 48 cows, all tawny and golden brown, with white speckles, moving amongst the beautiful soft green of the grass and the leaves. Two black and white cows added a nice definition and the bright brown of the red setter, Bray, jogging along behind, very pleased with himself on this rare occasion of being a farm dog, was a glorious spot of colour on the almost vivid purple of the track.

An old photograph showing the track where Anne cycled to work at New Park Farm.

An old post card showing the part of the Forest known as "Queen's Bower." Anne cycled through this magical spot every morning. She notes in her diary: "New Park House was built by Charles II for one of his favourite mistresses. It is mentioned frequently in the history of that period. He owned a great herd of deer for his pleasure and had "Queen's Meadow" cut in the middle of the Forest in order that they might be taken there and left to feed. Queen's Meadow and Queen's Bower were named after the Lady in Question." Anne, with other workers on the farm, herded the cows to Queen's Meadow for grazing.

We came to a tricky bit, where the cows must cross a bridge and into a gate into the meadow, a narrow bottleneck for such a large company. The boys shouted (and how picturesque they looked with their form jackets, blue berets log staffs and crimson faces), the cows mooed and the dogs barked and as they filed in through the gate, we counted to see they were all there. Joyce knows them all by name. I hope I shall some day. She told me the history of the place. New Park House was built by Charles II for one of his favourite mistresses and he spent a great deal of his time at New Park for this reason. It is mentioned frequently in the history of that period. He owned a great herd of deer for his pleasure and had the "Queen's Meadow" cut in the middle of the forest in order that they might be taken there and left to feed. The Queen's Meadow and the Queen's Bower were named after the Lady in Question. There are still deer in the forest and the men often see a white buck when they are driving the cows through in the early morning. Foxes too are here in numbers. Mr Gossling has lost 80 or so chickens this year killed by foxes.

I have been here 3 weeks today and in another week, I shall have passed through my baptism of fire and I hope I shall get my wages. I could kick myself for offering to work voluntarily for a month and scream each Saturday when I see the others all getting their crackly £1 notes.

Wednesday July 21

It rained all night and was still pelting when I got up at 6am. I was soaking by the time I got to the farm, caught Peter in the clover field, loaded up in a downpour and set off feeling very damp and rather miserable. However, the rain stopped and I gradually dried up and enjoyed some good canters on soft turf and did the round in record time. Joyce and Dorothy[14] were off, so it was all we could do to get through the milking in time. Old Joe was in a good mood and we had great fun and finished just as the Boss returned from the market. Eileen, Henry (the gypsy boy)[15] and I took the cows to Queen's Meadow, this time through a hazy forest dripping with rain, and leaves shining with water. It was very beautiful. I love this evening excursion and feast my eyes on the scene and love the noise of the cows and the shouting of the boys. Henry is a fascinating, leggy boy of 16, with an excellent straight nose and bow-like, laughing mouth. I can never understand a word he says, but I do like to look at him. His sister, Lizzie, a very handsome girl too, with a broad brown face, much freckled, with gleaming white teeth and an attractive conglomeration of gypsy clothes presented me with a bunch of honeysuckle. I'm afraid it was just "cupboard love", to induce me to give her my red scarf! I guessed this and afterwards was told that whenever she gives flowers, she proceeds to ogle for clothes. But my red scarf is too unduly admired for me to part with it lightly and I am afraid I have the honeysuckle and Lizzie has not my red scarf.

Mr Gossling and I have great jokes together about when "we go to prison" – and when the others will have to do all the work. I think he likes a joke and he is always amused to see old Joe being teased by the land girls as we milk. Joe hates to think we can do anything and finds fault wherever he can, but I think he's a good soul at bottom and always responds to a little frivolity. He adores his 4 year old son,[16] whom he waited 20 years for, a solemn, round-eyed little Joe the second!

Tarmac was a thing of the future in Avenue Road, Brockenhurst when this photo was taken in about 1920-30. For part of the war Anne's sister Vera lodged at 'Highfield' the house in the right hand corner of the photo. Vera moved to Brockenhurst to be near her husband, Marryat Dobie who in 1941 had been appointed as one of the first Training Instructors, Group B, Special Operations Executive, Beaulieu.

Friday July 23rd

General Farm Work

Returned to work once more feeling considerably refreshed after a day off, in which I did nothing except do odd jobs and potter – and see Vera off to Scotland – which left Brockenhurst sadly empty.

How to handle a heavy churn. It was jobs like this that used to be a male preserve.
(Illustration by Evelyn Dunbar)

Eileen has a sore hand and cannot milk, so I was bidden to stay behind while she did the round. I started the day by milking and then when the others were breakfasting, I cleaned the milk cooler, washed all the buckets and churns and had a good old clean up of the dairy, which had accumulated a lot of rubbish which I have been trying to get rid of ever since I came.

All morning, I brushed down cow byres (which is incredibly back breaking). Water must be carried about 300 yards in buckets from the drinking trough and two bucketfuls is a mere drop in those vast byres. I was exhausted by midday, but the byres were rewarding and really looked lovely, now showing red brick floors and the stalls layered with fresh straw. I felt I had really done a good day's work till the cows came in and two hours later, there was no sign that anything had ever been cleaned – and it will all have to be done again tomorrow. Oh dear! What a lot of things must be done every day, like washing up and dusting and it is so dull!

Saturday July 24

I must admit, I didn't much relish another day of byre-scrubbing. My limbs still ached and the thought of those byres almost made me weep. Imagine how relieved I was to see Eileen returning an hour after she had left walking and leading Peter. I knew "summat was up" and so it was. The bottom of the float had come out. I had been expecting it to happen for days and was thankful it waited till Eileen took over! They strung it together with a big chain and Mr Gossling sent me along too as Eileen would be so late, seeing it was Saturday and "payday."

I felt like an escaped schoolchild and sat up on top of the cans, hugging my knees with joy and soaking in the warm sun which I haven't felt for days.

We were terribly late and wickedly decided not to hurry, and get home too late to be put into any other job. We chattered and giggled and wandered along in the sunshine and talked to our friends and bought a bag of hot buns in the village and took turns in dishing out the milk and driving Peter. It was all great fun and we got home at 4.30pm in time to eat our lunch and take the cows along to Queen's Meadow. A nice day!

NEW PARK HOUSE

BUILT BY CHARLES II PROBABLY SOMEWHERE
ABOUT 1660. FOR A FAVOURITE MISTRESS.
NEW PARK IS STILL CROWN PROPERTY.

Remarkably Anne had the energy to write her diary after working dawn to dusk at the farm but she painted little. This watercolour of New Park House (see page 31), the 17th century manor house which was about four hundred yards from the farm buildings, was the fruit of a very rare opportunity.

Sunday July 25

I wakened late and hadn't time to make anything for my breakfast except tea. However, I arrived in good time and milked several cows, cleaned the dairy, etc and at 10am, Mr Gossling came along and said "You can take the afternoon off. We'll try and take turns at that every Sunday". I was thrilled but first decided to clean out the bicycle room, which is so choc-a-bloc with broken bottles and rubbish that it is most annoying. I did a grand job of work there and when the farm joint was being borne into the dining room, I made off on cycle and ate my bread and cheese in a field and sketched New Park House. Glorious to have escaped those byres for a second day!

I don't think I shall enjoy being on the farm all day as much as getting out on the road with Peter, where I am my own master. I shall miss driving and I shall miss my nice friends. I have many now! "A" Mess of course with Chopper and dear Jock and his cheery "Goodbye Anne love. See you tomorrow" and the nice railway man who walks along the line for his milk and the old man who has hunted over most counties in England and who never fails to stand

PEAS

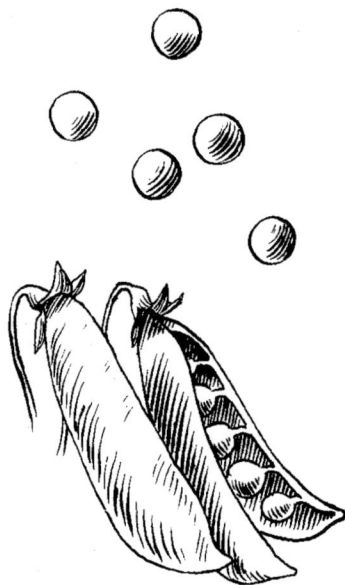

(Illustration by Evelyn Dunbar)

with his jug and pay me pretty compliments and tell me the day's news. Then old Mrs Giles, who gives me bundles of the "Times" – "to read and cut anything out I like" and the old lady who asked me to sit in her garden on my free day. She showed it to me and never have I seen a more perfect sight. The front of her house is plain and dull and very ordinary, but when she took me into her bedroom, which was completely filled with a large 4 poster bed, and I looked out of the window, I just could not believe my eyes. It was a paradise of colour and archways and beautiful green grass. A blaze of purple and crimson so perfectly set out that it took my breath away. She said modestly, "Yes, it is just at its best now" and I hardly want to see it again, perhaps less beautiful. Then there is my friend the dog who, the minute I lay down my can, he lays a large stone beside it for me to throw! And old Mr Mallaber, who gives me a lettuce from time to time, Mrs Bunning who does my laundry now and the old Mr Gulliver, who puts one pod of peas on the kitchen table for me – my ration – because he knows I love them.

Oh, I can't describe all those friendly faces that I see day after day. A few scowlers of course, but very few, and I shall miss them. However, it would be a pity not to do anything else and I am anxious to learn more about the farm. Jorgonson, the rival dairy – Brookley Farm Dairy – have offered me their job of Roundsman at 10 shillings more a week! But I shall stay where I am at the moment anyway.

I should never retire to this countryside. When I am in the Forest, I find beauty beneath those great trees and beside the little winding streams, but the Forest seen from outside is as monotonous and as depressing as a Malayan jungle. We have the same long, straight main roads, which cut through the forest for miles at a time, exactly like the Malayan roads cutting through jungle or rubber plantations and equally dull. The undergrowth of tall bracken and small bushes destroys the form of the larger trees and a dampness oozes everywhere. I long for open country and small hills and cornfields or ploughed land and a wide, distant skyline.

Even today cows, and occassionally ponies and donkeys, regularly stroll down Brockenhurst's Brookley Road, where Anne lodged. This postcard shows the street as Anne would have known it. She cycled from one end of it to the other every day. The second shop front from the right belonged to a "rival" dairy, Jorgonson's – Brookley Farm Dairy. They offered Anne a job with a higher salary. But she stayed at New Park.

Monday July 26th

A pleasant and peaceful day – milking and cleaning the dairy – Dorothy and Joyce were away bargain hunting at a salvage sale in Bournemouth and Eileen and Freda were out on the rounds, so I was left to my own devices and I did my work in a leisurely manner, just filling in the morning till dinner time. I sat in the sun in the garden for a while and felt very rested before I brought in the cows for milking. I milked eight. Then to Queen's Bower and home earlier than usual.

Tuesday July 27th

Byre scrubbing and bottle washing all day. I enjoyed the byre scrubbing better than the bottle washing. I found the former quite easy today. I even found it quite fascinating, but washing bottles is the one job I hate. The bath is just the wrong height (as is always a kitchen sink) and I get a kink in my back and feel miserable. Also, I never know if the bottles are really clean and am terrified of leaving any germs so take much longer probably than I need.

Another day off and a glorious one too. Hot sun in a cloudless sky from early morning "all the rich day through" till bedtime.[17]

I cycled to Lymington, a lovely ride, and lay at the sea's edge in the sun and swam in beautiful warm salt water at intervals. I had forgotten how lovely warm salt water is! – shades of Malaya. I swam and swam and swam and felt stretched and invigorated and then I lay and let the sun soak into my skin, while I gazed across the Solent to the misty island and watched an odd Invasion Barge move slowly through the blue water – the only sign of war. My bit of coast was quite deserted.

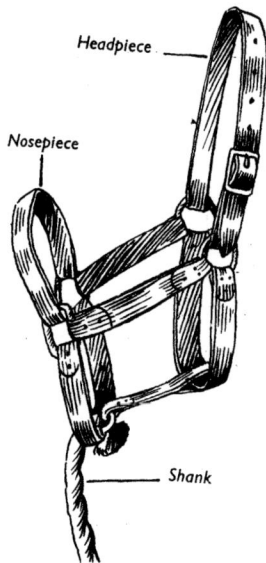

I love Lymington. Such beautiful old Georgian houses and gay sailors' cottages, almost side by side. I did some shopping, bought a marvellous pair of Industrial clogs for 2 coupons only and had a high tea at "Goodies" Tea Shop. Then I lay in a field on my way home and read and finally turned in about 9.30pm, feeling well and rejoicing!

Friday July 30th

The Milk Round Again – Eileen's Day Off

Peter had been turned out in the clover field without a halter, but I set out gaily with a tin of oats, a giant refreshed after my lovely day yesterday, determined to catch him. I did get him by the mane and held on like grim death, whereupon he swung round in a complete circle and swung me with him, like a clown at a circus, and flung me across the field – my nose and clean shirt – in the wet clover. Then of course he was off! And feeling slightly less commanding, I tried to cajole him with more corn. He came so far, but no further and meanwhile Danny, the Devil – angry because I wouldn't give her the corn – came behind me and landed me a hefty kick in the leg. I thought it was shrapnel! And feeling injured mentally and bruised physically, I

Headpiece

Nosepiece

Shank

HALTER

The halter is a headpiece like a bridle, but without a bit. To capture a horse or pony loose in a meadow – and Peter the pony could be very hard to catch – is easier said than done. But the official advice was clear. "Approach from the front," advises Michael Greenhill in *A Book of Farmcraft* "...with the halter in your left hand ready to slip over his head. It is important to keep all your movements calm and slow. Hold out your free hand and speak firmly... 'Whoa there, steady now!' Then lift your right hand unhesitatingly, grasp his forelock and slip on the halter; now you have control and may easily lead him away." But until the elusive, skittish Peter got to know and trust Anne, Mr. Gossling's comment remained true: "Peter is a woman-hater." Anne, however, could be as persuasive with ponies as she was with people. On the farm they all ended up good friends, perhaps Peter more than anyone. (Evelyn Dunbar illustration) went for help. Arthur, the old gypsy,[18] came but couldn't get near Peter so we drove him and finally I set off on the round, delighted to be in harness with Peter once more and on such a lovely morning.

All went well and I got home in good time, not feeling a bit tired. I really am getting over my aches at last and I felt so fresh in the evening that I asked if I might go to the "Park" to help with the harvest after supper.

The park looked most glorious – 300 acres of yellow corn, glowing in the golden evening sunshine, surrounded by great oaks and the reaper and binder carving its way through the tall oats with red and green wings moving in circles. How thrilled I felt to feel that here I was helping to secure Britain's food! I worked like a Trojan and Mr Gossling showed me how to stack up the sheaves in stooks (of 6 or 8 sheaves) so that the air can get through. Once the knack is learnt, it is quite easy and rhythmic, but the sheaves are about twice their normal size now, to save string, and therefore much more heavy and bulky. You work up 4 rows at a time, always walking from the back of the sheaves, as they are easier to lift that way. You take a bundle in each arm and swing each, stalks downwards, so that the ears prop up against each other, then give each a little push in the centre to make them firm, and two more similar pairs make a "stook". (See overleaf.)

In this way, the air can sweep through and it is much better that the round stooks so many people make. We worked till the dew began to fall and then came home feeling tired but well satisfied with a hot golden day, well spent.

& swing each, stalks downwards, so that the ears prop up against each other – then give each a little push in the centre to make them firm, & 2 more similar pairs make a "Stook".

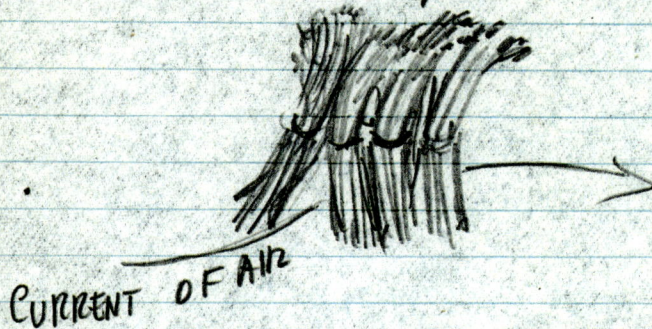

CURRENT OF AIR

In this way the air can sweep through – & it is much better than the Round Stooks so many people make –

We worked till the dew began to fall, & then came home feeling tired but well satisfied with a hot golden day, well spent!

SATURDAY. JULY 31st

"THE BATTLE OF THE FIELDS"!

The papers say that farmers & Land girls are fighting the Battle of

Anne wrote up her diary in long hand. The drawing on this page is the only instance in the whole diary of her using words alone. Although her writing flows easily, she is a careful selector of the right word. She is a great weaver of anecdotes, knowing exactly how much she needs to say.

Saturday July 31st

The Battle of the Fields

The papers say that farmers and land girls are fighting the "Battle of the Fields." We battled all day in the harvest fields and I loved it, but certainly I have battle scars – where thistles pricked even through my clothes. But it was glorious in the hot sun, with a light wind blowing which made the oats rustle and bend. Dorothy and Joyce and I worked together, four rows each, so we made quite a show of it. I got into a definite rhythm and didn't feel in the least tired. My new clogs are also excellent for the job as they press down the hard stubble and nothing can prickle my feet.

We drove home at dinner time with "Bray" on my knee and the old gypsy, Arthur, joggling along in the trailer behind. Then milking and herding the cows to the Queen's Meadow all eating apples which Sonny[19] shook down from a tree in the orchard – so warm with the sun they were, that they almost tasted like stewed apples.

Sunday July 31st

Another quiet day when we only did what work had to be done. The routine of milking, dairy cleaning, etc., and then we were free till the cows should be brought in after dinner. I sat in a field under a nice soft hay rick and wrote letters. A warm breeze was blowing which persisted in shooting down layers of hay on my head. Once or twice I was completely buried! It was pleasant and restful and when we all accumulated again for milking, we were in high spirits.

Monday August 1st

August Bank Holiday

Another Sunday-ish sort of day. Two of the men went off to Burley to the races, so we only did the necessary and I filled my spare time tidying up and sawing wood. Joyce washed my bottles for me because that is the only job I hate! And I got my first wages – £2-5/-. How proud I felt of them! And I can't really feel I deserve them when I enjoy everything so much. We were all in holiday spirits and had a great deal of back chat.

Tuesday August 2nd

Weeding Kale

Quite a change today. I was delighted when the morning's orders were being given out to hear Mary[20] being given the dairy to clean and "Anne to weed." I enquired "where?" and was told "On the left, past the Cowman's Cottages past the fields of purple flowering potatoes to the Kale. You will see tall white weeds and corn and a feathery bush. Pull all those out". I said yes very glibly but set off feeling very dubious as to whether or not I should know what to take out and what to leave in. However, there was no doubt at all when I reached the end of the potato fields (so pretty with a mauve and yellow-centred flower and sweetly scented), for there, beyond me, stretched about 8 acres of tall white hemlock, mixed with corn and a tall feathery weed which apparently is very prevalent this year. At the far end a good stretch had already been weeded, leaving the kale, almost a foot high, clean and green and flourishing, unchoked and luxuriating in the sunlight. There was a sharp, clear-cut line and I judged that one worked a row at a time. This was a job I knew I should enjoy. It was still early morning, with a nip in the air and a brightness in the sky which foretold a hot, sunny day later. I set to work with a will, pulling out great roots of hemlock in one hand and oats in the other. On and on I went, frequently looking back at the long row of kale I had freed to the light. It was most rewarding and most satisfying and the only difficulty was that I got an ache in the small of my back with bending hour after hour. Joyce and Dorothy came later and told me that we cut this kale in the winter (3 cartfuls of it a day) for the cows. This made the job for me more interesting than ever and we three "John Bull's Daughters"[21] took a row each and worked till dinner time. Then we went home, laden with milkwort for the rabbits.

After supper, I went to the park and stooked up corn till 9.30pm – a wonderful evening of golden light and long shadows stretching away from the stooks and the silence of evening when birds are hushed and no-one is about. I loved it.

A still from a Pathé newsreel of gypsies in the New Forest. Gypsies feature often in the Diary; an appealing, individualistic presence. Anne appreciates them and enjoys describing their independent character. At one point she calls them "a colourful gang" but she doesn't particularly romanticise them, as did some artists of the time. CREDIT: British Pathé Ltd.

Wednesday August 3rd

Weeding again, this time with the gypsies. I liked to watch them in their odd picturesque clothes. From time to time, they would gather in a bunch for a smoke and the assortment of colours is wonderful. Such fine, good looking women they are. And old Mrs Whitcher, a mother of 12, who has a baby of a few months and a granddaughter of a year, is the finest of them all. She has golden glowing skin, fine, clear-cut, delicate features and eyes two points of china blue. We chattered of this and that as we worked and I wondered how people with such a normal and civilised outlook can live in such an uncivilised way – like animals really, in a handful of filthy tents and yet they look wholesome and clean in themselves.

The old gypsy described admiringly by Anne. Whitcher was a fairly common gypsy surname.
CREDIT: Photograph by Stan Orchard

Milking after dinner, we all got very skittish and sang songs and spirits ran high. It is such fun, the vitality of these young things, so spontaneous and completely irresistible![22]

we are having a visitor this
week end. I rang up &
Mr Gosling says we can
have extra.
                M.P

Another doorstep note kept by Anne.

Friday August 5th

Returned to work refreshed after a free day which I spent pottering and getting ration cards, coupons, etc at Lyndhurst.

My day for the round – how I enjoyed it – out once more with Peter, in fresh air and sunshine – standing up in the float and rushing along. Everything went well and I was flattered when so many people said "We wish you'd always come, we like it when you come best". Old Mr Gulliver went especially up to his garden to pick me some peas.

The churns had their "shirts" on, damped to keep the milk cool. This was a lovely day out for me and it seemed no time before I had milked my evening cows, herded them up to Queen's Meadow, with a pocketful of apples and greengages (from the orchard) and jumped onto my bike for home.

Saturday August 6th

The boss took Dorothy and Joyce over to Milford for the day to lift the corn on his sister's farm there. So I was left to make things tidy for the weekend. I waved them away, feeling a little Cinderella-ish and said I'd look after things till they came back.

It was rather peaceful and nice cleaning the dairy and brushing down the yard at my own time and I did several cleanings-up which I have wanted to do since I came.

We got the cows in early and there was just Joe, Sonny and myself to milk. However, we got though pretty fast and then followed the usual Saturday evening rush! Everyone trying to get done and off as early as possible. The older men go to the pubs. And Sonny and the girls usually go to a dance. My routine is as weekdays. But the rush is infectious and I find myself breathless with excitement till I am on my bike and set for home.

August 7th to 22nd

Harvesting

A fortnight has passed with not one second in which to write my Journal. We have been harvesting and hard at it till 8 and 9 o'clock every night. It is now "black out" when I get home and all I can do is make a meal, prepare for the morrow, write my most necessary letters and get to bed – and Jove! I am glad when I'm there – after a solid 14 hours' work a day and no overtime!

I just have memories of glorious, long hot summer days spent in the harvest fields with corn stretching for acres all around and the great parkland trees behind. Corn being cut by the red and white reaper, driven by a man with no shirt and back as brown as the corn itself. Corn standing in stooks, and corn being made into ricks, with three great wagons pulled by the clumsy big cart horses. Loading the ricks – Joe, with a funny straw hat on, loading and unloading, the girls with dungarees rolled up above their knees and gay scarves round their heads, Sonny with his great, strong frame and crimson face, old Jack forever on top of the rick with the Boss, rather battered by lumbago but working steadily on and on without a murmur, the gypsies in a colourful gang "putting up" or "putting down" stooks, and in some far corner odds and ends of boy scouts, campers and parsons all lending willing and very efficient hands!

I did all the jobs in turn. When the corn is cut, it is first put up into stooks. You work up the rows so that the stalks face you. You work 4 rows at a time and take a sheaf under each arm and drop them simultaneously so that they fall against and prop each other up. Three of these pairs make a stook, or an aisle as the gypsies call them. They must be erected at even intervals and in nice straight rows. Oats is nice and light to stook, but wheat and barley are 10 times as heavy, especially when it is rather green and now more than ever as the sheaves are larger to save string.

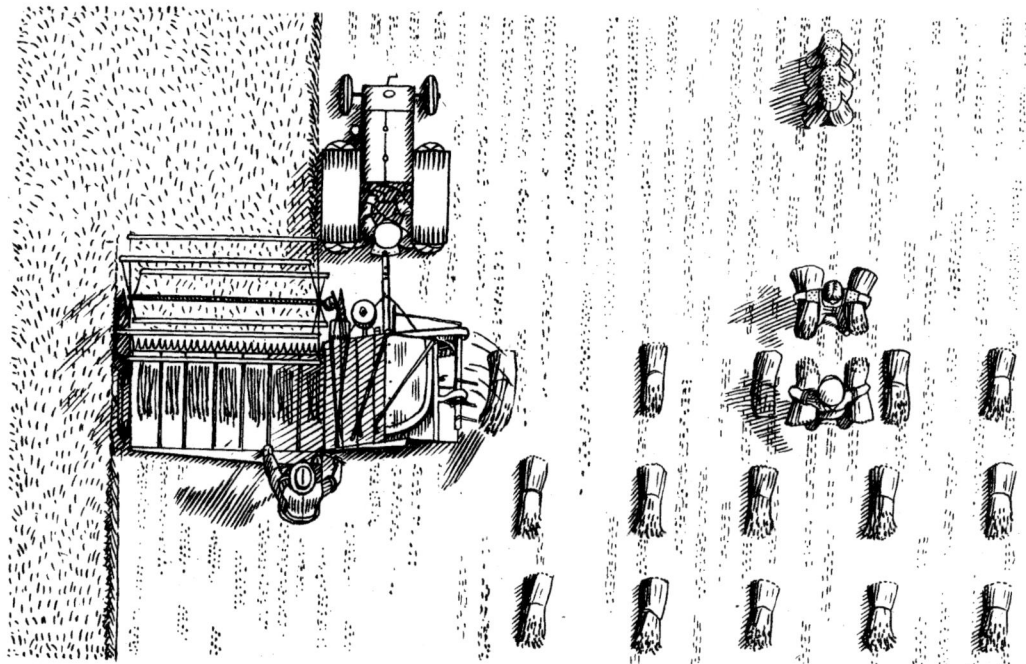

BINDER

This is one of Evelyn Dunbar's bird's-eye-view drawings in *A Book of Farmcraft*. It shows vividly how this period was a time when old and new farming practices were both employed. The binder could do a great deal of work, but workers were still needed to stook the sheaves. Mechanisation was gradually transforming agriculture, but Anne and the land girls were probably among the last farm workers to experience the heavy manual labour that had been the stuff of farming for centuries.

When the corn is ready to cart, the stooks must be pulled down. This is done with a prong and the sheaves are laid in rows wide enough apart for the wagon to drive between. The sheaves are always placed with their stalks facing the sun, or if there is no sun, the wind, for drying purposes, and also to make loading easier when they all face the same direction.

Now the wagon comes along with a small boy holding a great horse and a man on top to receive the sheaves and place them firmly so that a good high load may be stacked on. It makes all the difference to have a good wagoner and he gets higher and higher on top of the corn as we send up sheaves (ears first) on our prongs, points always downwards so as not to

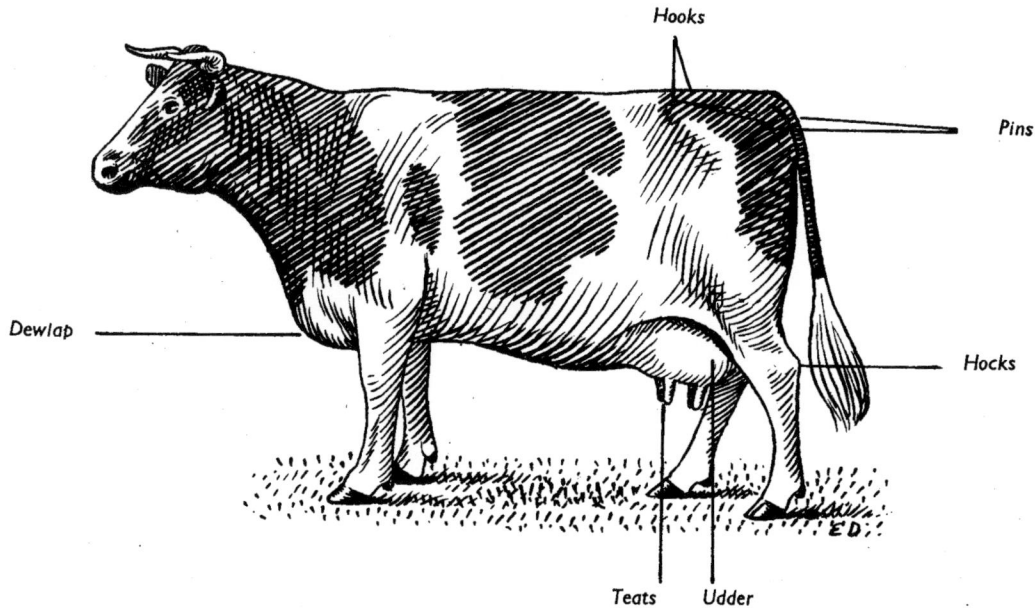

POINTS OF A COW

Girls coming from the cities sometimes didn't know one end of a cow from another.
But help was at hand in *A Book of Farmcraft*.
(Evelyn Dunbar illustration)

spike him. The boy at the horse's head calls "Steady there! Gee up" and on they move another few yards till the wagon is really complete and then it trundles away, rolling and swaying on the uneven stubble till it reaches the rick.

Loading the rick is the job I like best. Old Jack always builds the rick. He stands at the edge and places the sheaves, stalks outwards round and round, then into the centre, then out again. The man on the wagon throws up the sheaves to me, I pass them to the Boss who passes them to Jack who places them in position. So we go on and on, hour after hour, round and round the rick, getting higher and higher with a broiling sun pouring down and the dust from the corn getting into your eyes and down your throat. No sooner have we got rid of one wagon than another appears and sometimes they throw up the sheaves so fast there is hardly time to pass them on. Sonny is a splendid rhythmic worker. Not too fast, not too slow and how quickly you can get on that way. It is wonderful what slow steady effort achieves. The countryman's movements are so slow, but they are untiring and can go on hour after hour and never slacken the pace. The townsman wastes the last few hours of every day by being tired with over exertion and too much hurry.

I loved working in the fields till late, but milking afterwards I find wearing in the extreme. There is nothing I dislike so much as milking when I am tired. Cows seem to me like children – the more impatient you are with them, the more troublesome they become! Each one needs different handling. There is the fidgety cow who refuses to stand still, who dances about on her hind legs, who keeps edging away from you or pushing you out with her tummy. There is the cow who kicks and you must keep your eye on her, for any moment her hoof may land on your knee, in your bucket or in your stomach! There is your own cow and the cow behind you who lash their tails like a whip across your face and more usually than not, right in your eye! That is sheer agony and happens again and again on a hot summer's day when flies are thick on the cows and also on your own arms and legs. It is difficult to keep patient, especially when you have a cow whose teats are so small and tight you can't get a hold of them or so large and fat you can't get hold of them, or so low to the ground that you have to bend nearly double to get down to them. And then there are the cows who "hold back" their milk and all you can do is to wait and hope for the best, while you see the others moving on while you are left far behind.

As I say, it all needs great patience, which is very often lacking at the end of a long hot day. Once or twice, old Joe and I were the only two milking, 48 cows between us. But we generally struck up a few good old songs and went through our repertoire which always sounds more tuneful to the accompaniment of milk swishing into a pail (like water running into a bath) and the Boss would come home and say "Anne and Joe singing again."

Then there are the cows to be let out, the sheds to brush down, the pails to wash, the cooler to clean, and hey presto, then I jump on my bike and am off like a streak across the moor, which is now purple with heather and the air is so laden with honey I can almost taste it. And then I open my paper and read "Bumper Harvest" – "the leaning ears of wheat are astir with rumours of Victory" and I feel gratefully tired that I have really been able to help.

But today has been wet and work has ceased. We have got up 68 acres of corn and have about 58 more to see us through. Two or three weeks more of fine weather will finish us, but the skies are grey and lowering and it looks very much like a hold up which is disappointing.

Sunday August 29th

A week later

Yes, there has been a hold up this week. We have tried valiantly and put up or pulled down hours upon end, hoping the rain would keep off for another day or so, but we have had nights of heavy rainfall and the wheat became so heavy that it was only fit for the men to "carry" – we girls did the milking and cleaned the cowsheds and kept the Farm Front going very successfully. One morning I did the dairy and cleaned and washed two cowsheds and cleaned the paddock all myself. I felt very pleased with myself, and not awfully tired.

I have been here exactly 2 months today and this morning when I looked at my 2 gallon pail, brimming over with lovely frothy milk (from one cow), I felt I had really achieved quite a lot. I remember the lifeless dribble of milk I got at the beginning and how I used to envy those frothy pails. Freda started to milk today and I was amused to find myself "stripping" her cow for her with the assurance of an expert.

I have certainly learnt a lot and the more I know about cows, the less I like them! They are quite the most obstinate, stupid and annoying creatures under the sun. When I get them to myself in a large field, I shout all Joe's swear words at them, and a few of my own as well, and that makes me feel better. Joe laughed today and said "Anne said when she first came, I love cows. Now she thinks different and swears at them, same as I do. But she be a proper old cow hand now, be Anne!"

I feel as if I have been here for years. I love the variety of each day, no two days are ever alike and you can never say "Tomorrow I shall do this" because you just never know what tomorrow may bring. I also like the FUNCTIONAL-NESS of farming – it is so "big" and all done for a purpose. There is nothing finicky or pernickety about it. Nothing is just done "to look nice". It is all done for a reason. Corn is stacked in a certain way to let the air through. Stooks are built in rows, a certain width to facilitate loading the wagon. The dairy things are washed in 3 waters – 1. in cold to loosen the milk 2. in hot to wash away the grease and 3. in cold to close up the pores of the metal quickly and keep out the dust. Even the cowsheds are cleaned every day because if they weren't, you just couldn't cope with them. There is a reason for everything and I like the nice, big, honest to God tools you use – great brushes and spades and even clumping about in heavy clogs makes me feel like sweeping!

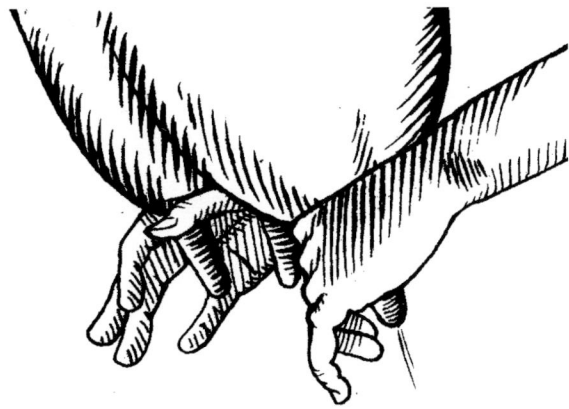

STRIPPING

Stripping is a skill that takes practice. It means making sure that the udder is completely dry with no last trickles to come. At the outset Old Joe showed Anne how to do it; and later, when Freda started milking at New Park, Anne demonstrated her own acquired stripping ability with some panache!

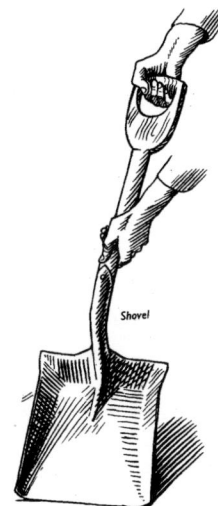

One thing Anne most definitely had in common with Evelyn Dunbar, though there is no evidence they met, was a love of tools – particularly hefty farm tools. "I like the nice, big, honest to God tools" Anne wrote in the diary. Dunbar's strong black and white style in *A Book of Farmcraft* is the visual equivalent of Anne's comment – calling a shovel a shovel! (Evelyn Dunbar illustration)

One day, two calves were born down in the Park[23] and we were sent to bring them and the heifers home. We drove them about 3 miles back and, of course, the silly cows insisted on walking in all the most awkward places. Their little calves (2 days old) tottered valiantly behind their mothers, but as we reached the Long Meadow, their legs got weak and very wobbly and so in the end we carried them across our shoulders. They were tucked up in nice clean straw for a day or so beside their mothers, but now they are sold for veal. The Boss took them away in a trailer to Ringwood Market where they fetched about 30 shillings apiece. We have another one now and several more to come.

I am to do the round tomorrow for a week – and today Peter walked off when Eileen was in a house, turned a corner and she found him and the float both turned over on their backs and she had to get the harness CUT OFF. I wonder how I shall fare tomorrow?

WEEK	WEEK BEGINNING	MIERS ROUND	SWAY RD. ROUND	FARM.	WASHING BOTTLES Etc
1	30 Aug	ANN	AILEEN	FREDA	ANN
2	6 Sept	ANN	AILEEN	FREDA	AILEEN
3	13 Sept	ANN	FREDA	AILEEN	FREDA
4	20 Sept	ANN	FREDA	AILEEN	ANN
5	27 Sept	AILEEN	FREDA	ANN	AILEEN.
6	4 Oct	AILEEN	FREDA	ANN	FREDA.
7					
8			ANN		

The milk rota.

Monday 30th August to Thursday 2nd September

Back on the Round

Four nice days out with Peter again. The first day old Joe set me up with a conglomeration of harness, which really wasn't too bad and it was with a lovely sense of freedom that I set off down the wide avenue, under the ancient oaks, leaving New Park behind me and cowsheds and dairies and sweepings and milkings! The morning air was crisp and bright and I felt a feeling of autumn. The fields beneath the oaks were now stubble with golden corn ricks standing neatly stacked ready for thrashing. What a short time it seems since they were luscious with thick grass, clover and ox eye daisies. And yet, what a lot of work has been put into them since those early June days when I made my first appearance. Haymaking then harvest and today we have had our first day of ploughing. Ploughing the small barley field

New Park farm as it was in the 1940s, a straightforward working farm. Today the dairy at New Park that Anne came to know so well has been demolished. Cows, pigs and workhorses have all gone, and there are certainly no hens scratching away in the yard. New Park is now the showground for The New Forest and Hampshire County Show.

down in the Park and we are still carrying the wheat up at the farm – as the Countryman's Diary expressed it: the end and the new beginning of a perpetual epic.

As I drove on, I noticed how red the berries had grown, odd stalks of bracken gleamed out yellow amongst the sea of green and, in one garden, a maple tree was positively crimson. Flowers are now yellow and tawny as opposed to the pink of the rose season, yellow daisies and chrysanthemums predominate – they grow in thick masses interspersed with mauve and purple michaelmas daisies.

My first day was uneventful, but rather lengthy as I had not quite got into my stride again, and Eileen, the little wretch, had taken no money on Saturday or Sunday. She knew I was taking over, so left it for me! "The other young lady said she was in too great a hurry to wait" my customers said, so I shackled in £7 or £8, and of course that all took time.

Next morning also, Eileen and I came to blows. She was bottling up the milk instead of Freda (who is milking now) and she tried to send me out with about half my quota, in order to keep lots for herself. "You can cut your customers down by hundreds" she said angrily. But I notice when they were her customers, she made enough fuss and said they were all down to their rations! So I stuck to my guns and helped myself. And set off feeling irritated and out of tune with everything. Ten minutes out, Peter jerked forward and I felt a loosening of the reins and lo and behold, his breast strap had broken and his whole harness slipped below his flanks. He started to kick his hind legs and I thought the cart would go for six. However, I steadied and unharnessed him and led him home again to old Joe, who once more repaired the damage with odd buckles and pieces of string. He came back with me to the cart to harness up and find the pin out of the left wheel and the whole wheel just about off! In another hour or so, it most undoubtedly would have been off. How we do take our life in our hands in these contraptions. However, I had a pleasant round, pretty well made up for lost time and washed all the bottles when I got back. 200 bottles and churns and buckets etc is bad enough in itself, but as well, there is the fire to make up and constantly attend to, the milk cooler "to watch" and all the various cowmen's wives and gypsies to dole out milk to in the dairy. The fire is the greatest plague. It burns under the boiler to heat the water and is fed by wood from the stack yard. Either it won't burn at all or else it roars away and burns whole tree trunks at the rate of knots.

Today I had a row with a customer who left no jug out, so I left no milk. Her door was locked and her neighbour was out also, so I assumed she was away. Was she furious?! "That's a poor excuse! That's a poor excuse!" she shouted as I tried to explain matters. "Because of you, my children had no milk". "Because you forgot to put your jug out, I think you mean" I said, as I jumped onto the float and drove off and all the way down the road I heard her yelling and screaming "I'll write and tell Mr Gossling about you, I will" and I thought that really (even more than cows), an irate woman is the most disagreeable object in the whole world. And I expect I shall have another to deal with tomorrow, one I left a note for under her jug to say that if she didn't leave her money, I could leave her no milk. She is forever grumbling about the milk and never pays.

will the Milk Lady please wait

Another doorstep note Anne kept. Her customers addressed her as "the milk lady." This would have not dismayed Anne, though a debate recorded later in the Diary as to whether or not she was a "lady" caused her great amusement. Old Joe had the final word on the subject.

I saw a cow with a wooden cage on its shoulders to stop it breaking through hedges. It looked so funny in the distance, as if it had immense horns.

September 2nd to 12th

Ten more days on the round. Some have been pleasant and passed quickly enough, others seem unending, as if I should never get through. I have noticed patches of yellow appearing on the trees, but these last two days have been sunshiny and balmy, with beautiful blue skies; almost cloudless. Sunshine and the capitulation of Italy have made everyone's spirits rise and milk is now no longer of major importance. Even when it turns sour I am told almost impersonally!

One nice morning when I was feeling gay, I drew up alongside a telephone repair car. The driver looked into my float and said: "Any eggs to spare today?" As it happened, I had an extra allocation of 2 or 3 dozen and several duck eggs as well. He saw them, so when I answered: "Oh no, not for you" he took no heed and got down from his car to show me what he had in his pocket. "Look" he said, "at this wonderful rasher of gammon – for my breakfast – but I've nothing to fry with it. Haven't you just one egg?" As I looked at the red and succulent rasher, a vision rose in my mind of it spluttering in a frying pan with a large egg alongside and I thought of my grumbling old Mrs Gulliver and Mrs Reeves and I was sure this nice man deserved it more. "Here's a duck egg," I said. "You must pay me 2d for it and on your life don't tell a soul or I'll get the sack." "Mum's the word", he replied, his eyes gleaming. "I'll pay you a shilling for it if you like." The egg was hastily transferred from my box to his pocket, beside his gammon. And as I drove away, I felt the windows of all the houses in Beaulieu Road dark and cadaverous looking. They gaped at me knowingly, and guiltily I whipped Peter along and out of sight. But my conscience would not be still – the more I thought of it, the more criminal I felt. It was really a dreadful thing to do and if it were spread abroad Mr Gossling might think I made a practice of that sort of thing, so I plucked up my courage and I confessed. "I sold one of your customer's eggs to a telephone man in the road," I said. "I thought he would appreciate it more than those grumbling old women." And I explained about the rasher of gammon. The Boss grinned and said: "Yes, I'm sure, and I expect you think the less Mrs Gulliver has, the less she has to grumble about." We both laughed and feeling very relieved I walked away saying "I won't do it again." And he said: "No, be a good girl next time!!"

Today I was not a good girl. I forgot to turn on the water in the cooler and when my churn was all roped onto the float and I was just about off, Eileen said, "The milk's warm." And so it was. It all had to be run through again – 15 gallons of it – and I was very disappointed as I had risen extra early so as to be off in good time.

I am given the most luscious pears and plums and apples as I wend my way. I've never eaten so much fruit before. One woman gave me sweet corn, which was scrumptious boiled for my supper and eaten with melted butter all running down my chin.

September 14, 15, 16

Three Days Leave in London Town followed by 10 Days on the Round

It was with the greatest excitement that I left the farm on Tuesday evening, all set for my 3 days Harvest Holiday in the great capital. And every second of it merited my excitement and anticipation – from the moment when I arrived at my club and the nice door porter said, "You look like a bit of harvest yourself, Madam, if I may say so" till the final twenty minutes when I was rushing for the "Last Train" and just caught it by the skin of my teeth arriving home at 3am to be up again by 6.

It was grand to see my friends, so unchanged, and so very congenial; to see the old familiar buildings which I knew so well, to wander through the streets in and out of the shops, to have good things to eat and to be abed in the mornings till I felt the urge to rise. I felt 100% fit and on the crest of the wave all the time. It was one of those holidays when everything went just right.

An old postcard of the watersplash in Brockenhurst from the late 1940s. Anne would have cycled through this shallow ford on her bicycle on her way to work at New Park Farm. If it was flooded, she would have crossed by footbridge.

And yet, when I cycled across the moor, white with frost, on Friday morning, I could not regret my return to work and to routine. I felt that indeed my lines were set in fair places[24] – everything looked beautiful in the golden morning sunlight, with a blue sky. The old farmstead looked peaceful and serene and continuing. I felt proud that I was part of it and that I had part ownership in those cows grazing in the dairy field and the great cart horses and the little round ponies. I thanked the Boss for my "nice holiday" which seemed to please him enormously and then I got off on the Round with Peter. We rushed through the bright sunlight in complete unison and, enormously exhilarated, I have felt a deep feeling of peace ever since. For 10 days, I have done the Round most joyously, most of them golden autumn days with frost in the mornings and a hot soaking sun later in the day, with blue skies and a sense of maturity and fulfilment felt only in autumn.

THE MOOR BETWEEN BROCKENHURST & MY FARM.

This is the cover for the second half of her Diary. The postcard she chose is a typical New Forest scene – common land with ponies, pools or streams of water, a few trees, well cropped grass, gorse, heather. She calls it "the moor." When she cycled from Brockenhurst to the farm every day, such open land was on her right, while on her left was ancient woodland. The words "New Forest" cover both kinds of landscape, not just trees. Walking this route today, not much appears to have changed since Anne was here six or seven decades ago.

Yesterday was the harvest thanksgiving parade for Land Girls at Winchester. It was disappointing that I couldn't go too, but only right that the others who are WLA should go instead of me. They marched with a band through the town and attended a service in the cathedral. Lord Wavell,[25] whose family has lived in Winchester for over 500 years, read the lesson and the Bishop gave an address. How I should have loved it and I felt slightly ironical when I found the great excitement of their day was coming home in a luggage van with some sailors!!

Today also was the Battle of Britain Thanksgiving Service – the N.F.S.[26] – the Civil Defence, A.R.P.[27] etc., paraded to the old church. I saw them all while I was delivering my milk and I longed to go too. Mr Gossling said: "You should come too. One of the girls would lend you a Land Army badge, or you could write a notice 'Too old, but useful' !! and I added 'Very useful you mean.'"

My month on the Round is over. Now I start my fortnight on the farm.

St Nicholas Church, Brockenhurst. The church stands at the top of a hill on the road from Lyndhurst to Lymington. A Saxon church had been on the site before it, and the Domesday Book records a church here. Anne mentions her regret at not being part of the Battle of Britain Thanksgiving Service at the church in September 1944 – she was not an official member of the Women's Land Army. She saw the parade as she went on her milk round.

My Fortnight on the Farm – Potato Lifting

There had been a great deal of talk about potato lifting, which everyone seemed to dread, when we were harvesting. Old Arthur's pet comment was "This is nothing, just you wait till we starts potato lifting – acres and acres of it. That'll break your back good and proper!" So it was with mingled anticipation and awe that I looked forward to this fortnight. I was anxious to have it behind me, but I was not sure how I should shape in this most dreaded of all jobs. As it turned out, I had only one day of it. Apparently, we were waiting for the "spinner" to come and shoot them out, but the spinner was delayed, so I started off with a week of easy placid days just cleaning the dairy equipment, feeding the calves and cleaning out the bull. It was all very pleasant after the excitement of the round and I had the farm to myself, save for old Joe who did the cowsheds day after day.

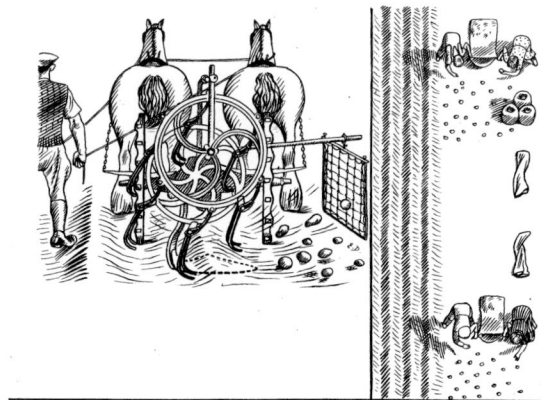

POTATO SPINNER—AND PICKERS AT WORK

Walter Gossling hired a potato spinner, but gathering the potato crop still involved hard manual labour. Evelyn Dunbar's drawing is a distinct, easily understood description of a complex machine.

57

We would meet at the trough to fill our buckets from time to time and have a few minutes' chatter. Eileen and Dorothy were doing the rounds, Freda was away and Joyce would spend the day down at the Park on the tractor. I used to envy her, when I thought how I should like to see the furrows I had ploughed and how thrilling it must be to plough up a stubble field and then to sow it and then to see the lines of pale green and know it was all my doing. But when I saw her return in the late afternoon, covered with oil and grease, looking grey with grime and tiredness and deaf from the noise of the engine, I decided she could have the tractor and I was well enough off where I was.

Carol would "help" (or hinder!) me all morning.[28] She would be waiting for me when I came from milking. "Can I help you to clean the dairy now Anne?" she would ask, with her little head on one side and her bright eyes sparkling. It was impossible to refuse her and although she held up proceedings considerably, she was an interesting companion and wise beyond belief for her four years. She has watched us doing all these jobs all her young life and knows how they should be done. She is allowed to milk one cow in the afternoons and there she sits, a minute object, on her tiny stool underneath old General, pulling with her little fat hands for all her might! She will wash her first and then swear at her if she thinks General's holding back her milk and bang her in the udder in the approved style, if Joe's swear words fail to have the desired effect. She knows the names of mostly every cow, even out in the fields, which to me is a miraculous achievement.

Anne had observed the milking process long before she came to New Park to do it herself. This drawing of a very small girl milking a very large cow is from her German trip sketchbook, 1926.

I just know most of them in the cowsheds in their order, but outside, they are a maze and I can only tell a few outstanding ones like "Panda", who has white circles round her eyes, "Magpie", who is black and white and "Jane" whose horns grow straight up from her head. I hate to show my ignorance, so I call out "Come on Dora, come on Primrose" which is pretty safe as we have several Doras and several Primroses, who will all look exactly alike to me. I love to watch Carol herding these great cows, running after them, a quaint little figure dressed usually in tight, shrunken dungarees and tiny Wellingtons, a bright little bow tied at the top of her dark, curly head and some gay coloured jersey whose arms have receded above the elbows with much washing. She will brandish a great stick and whack them on, perfectly fearless, and at the same time so sensible and so obedient. She is unfailingly there to meet the "Round Girls" come back, so that she may have a ride from the stables to the field. "Just in time for a ride, aren't I Anne?" she says every day and I answer yes, knowing well that she has been waiting a good hour to be "just in time!" She sits up on Peter as pleased as punch and kicks her heels into his sides to hurry him up. Then we give him a carrot and make up stories "of what he will say to Danny" when he returns to her. He usually first rolls on his back and kicks his four legs in the air and then he will stand close to Danny really as if he were telling her the news of the day. The two ponies are devoted and will stay side by side for hours on end.

When Carol "helps" me in the dairy, I insist that she wears an apron, a long one made of fancy oilcloth and she is never allowed to touch the taps or the hose. She dabbles away in the buckets, chattering hard and singing at the top of her voice. Her conversation is a string of questions which don't seem to require answers and she is so happily occupied that I feel the slight inconvenience she causes me is worthwhile.

When we have finished the dairy, we feed the calves. Five different lots needing five different diets – warm milk, cake, or cake and crushed oats, water and hay. I still marvel at their strength. One quite young calf can knock me down and when fifteen of them come round and buffet and butt at me with all their strength, it requires all my skill to empty the bucket of milk into the trough and escape undamaged.

After the calves comes Ferdinand or "Billy the Bull". I am quite fearless of him now and deal with him without a tremor. Carol will hold his pole while he drinks from the trough and I stand and watch this superb illustration of ignorance, where he knows not his strength nor she her weakness. One day I admit I did hurry him back to his shed, when the sirens sounded and aircraft flew low overhead and I had a sudden weird picture in my mind of bombs dropping in the yard, with Ferdinand at the end of a pole.

When his shed was nicely cleaned out, we would gather logs and build a good fire under the boiler for the bottle washing after dinner and take our dinner hour ourselves.

Before artificial insemination kicked in, the bull was an essential part of a dairy farm's stock. Not all bulls were difficult or aggressive. This New Park bull is behaving itself, even if the three land girls display a certain tentative respect for the beast. Furthest from the bull in the photo is Dorothy Gossling, Walter and Kate's only child, who with her husband Andrew Korbey was to farm New Park for many years. Next in line is Freda Sque, who married and emigrated to Canada. But the identity of the bravest girl remains unknown. She might be "Joyce" who certainly features in the diary, though without a surname.

Nothing rushed or strenuous about this routine and I welcomed it and felt more rested each day. On Thursday, to relieve any possible monotony, the vet arrived to inoculate 13 young heifers against abortion (a germ prevalent in these parts, which can be caught from the grass and which is very infectious). They had been driven up from the Park and were herded in the cowshed. The vet laid out his little bottles of serum in rows on a stack of straw in the paddock and Joe and Sonny caught the heifers in turns and held them ready for the vet to inoculate. It was a veritable Rodeo! and required tremendous strength and skill on the men's part to get them into position and hold them steady. They would catch them by both horns, prise their heads upwards and hold them there with one hand, gripping right between the nostrils. There were several amusing scuffles on the slippery cowshed floor and once Sonny was dragged several yards on the flat of his back in thick manure. When the vet inserted his needle low in the heifer's neck, she would plunge and rear and kick and one actually forced her way into the paddock, whence she took a leap, right over the rows of little bottles and landed clear with no damage done. How we laughed!

After dinner, we drove them back to the Park. Five of us went and none too many, for they were very troublesome and took the wrong turning every time. One leapt the tall iron fence and refused to leap back. We chased her through dozens of fields and finally had to take her up through the forest till we met the main road. At length, we reached the "Park," where I had not been since harvesting days, and I could hardly believe my eyes to see those golden harvest fields now a vista of newly ploughed earth, with long furrows stretching up over the hilly parts and some already sowed with winter wheat. How swift is the cycle of the seasons and how beautiful it all looked on this mellow afternoon with massed foliage, turning to yellow and orange, contrasted so vividly against the depth of the dark soil. We climbed to the top of the hillside and from there, I found the finest view I have had around here – I saw ridges of forest stretching for miles and miles, getting fainter in the distant haze of the late afternoon. Above, the sky was blue, birds sang and aircraft raced overhead. I looked at these ploughlands and wondered if I should be here to reap their harvest and whether or not the world would be at peace?

Dropping over the other side of the hill, we came upon the Boss driving his tractor, turning over furrow after furrow of stubble ground. He was to take us home, so obediently he stopped, covering the tractor with a gorgeous orange tarpaulin, tied it down, gave us each an oil can to carry and then drove us home to tea, the boys swinging in the trailer.

October 6th

Potato Lifting at Last

Frosts were heavy and the Boss began to worry about his potatoes. "We'll have to plough them out" he said "till the spinner arrives." So old Arthur the gypsy was sent off with the small horse plough and got busy. I hurried up with my work and made my way to the potato field eager to find out what I should do. All the gypsies were there before me. It was a grey day and the scene I saw was like a painting of the Angelus[29] – groups of grey figures bending over the grey brown soil, with rows of filled and bulging sacks placed across the fields at intervals and empty buckets waiting to be filled.

A newcomer was a good excuse for a chat. The gypsies stopped their work, pulled the ever-ready cigarettes from their pockets, lit up and gathered round for a gossip. They work hard and fast when they do work, but so often they stop to smoke and to gossip that it is tantalising to conjecture how much work they could do if they kept at it.

"What do I do?" I asked.

 "You take a bucket from over there and fill it either with 'eaters' or seed potatoes. The bad 'uns and the small 'uns, you throw over the row for the pigs" said Sarah,[30] who is always willing to instruct.

I decided to collect 'eaters' – the large, good quality potatoes and I soon learnt how I must scoop under the soil to find them all. We worked in groups along the rows, hurriedly in order to clear the last row before Arthur should come round again with his plough.

When our buckets were full, we filled our sacks and when our sacks were full, George[31] came with the wagon and carted them to the stables, where he laid them on a bed of straw and carefully latched the doors to prevent the pigs (who are now loose to pick up acorns which lie in profusion everywhere) from entering.

I felt there was a lack of method in the way we worked and I should like to know the proper procedure. The gypsies are incapable of any system. They can only work in groups all in a huddle. I never really got down to it and the next day I was off on the round again.

Wednesday morning, I was dragged from "under a cow" to do the round as Eileen, who had been on her way to work, phoned to say she had a pain and had gone home again.

My instant reaction was of slight resentment. I was enjoying this less strenuous life and didn't relish being vested from it. But the minute I was off with Peter, my spirits rose. I had forgotten the pleasure of driving him and the exhilaration of clattering along the frosty roads feeling his response to my hand and whip (which I flicker over his back pretending I cast a fly at a certain spot). It was lovely.

One stretch of forest isolated itself as a gorgeous tapestry; the dull green of oaks meeting the undergrowth of tall fronded bracken, bright green, yellow, brown and gold. This must surely have been the ancient motif for a hundred tapestries and now we say "How like a tapestry" just as we liken a brilliant (probably blood red) sunset to a postcard.

It was a gorgeous day, October at its best, and here they call it St Luke's Little Summer, because the weather about St Luke's day is generally sunny and warm.

The schoolchildren were home for a fortnight to help with the end of the harvest and I felt like the Pied Piper. Wherever I went, they came rushing along beside and behind me. With screams and shouts, flutterings of arms and legs as they tried to race my float. Such a medley of colours, gay reds and yellows darting beneath the golden beeches, with shafts of golden light gleaming across auburn heads. How they chattered. Their gaiety was infectious. I found myself shouting and becoming quite skittish and Peter also obviously was excited with this wild procession. He would canter along in grand style as if he knew it was a race and he enjoyed it. I remarked about this to Eileen and she said "Well of course, he was a children's riding pony before the Boss bought him you know".

For a day or so, Whitley Ridge was empty and deserted. The Marines (Chopper and Jack & Co) have moved on and there was a gap before the Canadians[32] came to replace them. When they did arrive and saw the float drive into the yard, there was an uproar. They came clamouring for milk and when I poured it into their jugs, they would drink a pint off in one gulp! Milk is the thing they have missed in this country more than anything else and to the Colonel's Batman it spelt HOME for he has worked on a dairy farm in Canada all his life. He was amused beyond telling at the way we deliver it privately and most interested to know our whole system of milk production. The greatest difficulty they have to deal with over there is cooling the milk and keeping it cold during the summer. They are not allowed to sell any milk which is not pasteurised and he agrees with the Boss that it destroys about 1/3rd of its value and reduces its cream. He thought our milk tasted "just wonderful."

The chef is a French Canadian, who cannot speak one word of English. For several days, I remained dumb with him, feeling trepidations at using my rusty French. But one day when I was on the crest of the wave, I suddenly became loquacious – and was he thrilled! He rushed into the kitchen and excitedly conveyed to the others that I was "a French lady". It was a great success. I have seen all their photographs of their children, little fur-clad figures in deep snow, some three years old whom they have never seen and I tell them about John and we have a great bond of sympathy.[33]

The forest is now teeming with Commandos. They look very dare-devil with their rakish green berets and one of their chief delights is to shout after me and taunt me. Once, just as I was turning into the Avenue, a group asked for a lift. I whipped up Peter but they ran behind and as I broke into a canter, one jumped up behind me and together we swept out into the coach yard, where the men and Freda were unloading potatoes. How surprised they were. And how they teased me. "And you a married woman too Anne. Well, I never!"

They are encamped all around Queen's Bower and we have to drive our cows right through their camp in the evenings. They are generally cooking their "Tea" and are thus in high spirits and jeer at us and ask cheeky questions! One evening, a great pig from the forest[34] attached itself to our cows and wandered along with them. A great lout of a soldier asked me if it were ours and when I said "No" he said rather fearfully "Is it a wild one?" At this point a very pale faced, supercilious young officer stepped forward and with devastating irony said "Does it look like a wild pig – IDIOT!!"

Another day, when I was washing the bottles, two Commandos wandered into the yard. They walked up and down, evidently concentrating deeply. They peered into all the outhouses and barns and seemed to be searching. But what for? I could contain my curiosity no longer. I went out and enquired. They each held a piece of paper with a list of things written on it and they divulged that they were out on a "treasure hunt" and were looking for (in the farmyard) a nail, 2 white feathers and 2 horse's hairs. They had found the nails and when I

Parts of the New Forest become flooded as rivers overflow after heavy rainfall. Photograph by Tony Johnson.

conducted them to the fowl house, they soon found their feathers. But where oh where could they find 2 horse's hairs? I pointed to the meadow and said "Well there are 4 horses, it's EASY." They stared incredulously and asked "But how can we get them?" "Pull them out" I answered "– out of their tails". They gaped, horror-stricken at such an idea. But when they looked again at their lists, the urgency of their quest came over them and together they went boldly into the field and did their worst!

Ten days we owed to St Luke[35] for his "little summer" and I thanked him for them daily. They were unforgettable days when the forest was no longer a mass of monotonous green, but a burning glory of red and yellow and gold. The sun shone in blue skies, there was no wind and for ten days, leaves dropped silently and steadily, spots of yellow light dropping to the ground. It was incredibly peaceful, this falling of leaves in silence and gradually the roadways grew carpeted yellow and gold and the sound of Peter's hooves were dulled by the soft leaves. The children had returned to school, so there was a feeling of great calm. Bit it was, alas, the calm before the storm. St Luke's Little Summer was followed precipitously by a week of torrential rain. The Equinoctial gales it was now, I was told, but whatever it was, it came down in lumps. I would be soaked before even I reached the farm in the mornings and I would stand in the float all day with the heavens emptying themselves upon me till I felt there just could be no more rain left.

Yet day after day followed exactly the same. The rivers filled and flooded into the forest and onto the roads. We had to make detours to avoid the floods. The farmyard became a morass of mud. Everything was soaking and everyone was soaked. The wood was so wet that we couldn't build a fire in the boiler room without being smoked-out. Day after day, I washed bottles, sick and choking with smoke, with tears running down my cheeks. And still the rain pelted down and our tempers became more frayed. One man alone was unperturbed. I met him sheltering under a tree in a downpour and he said cheerfully "One thing's certain, we can't stop it" and I realised how futile it was to rant and to roar when we should surely just have to wait till it decided to stop.

It did stop at last, but that was a bad day for me because I dropped my mackintosh off at the back of my cycle on my way to work. The float was loaded and I was ready to set off when I discovered this, so I threw a coat over Peter and rushed madly back again across the moor. It was nowhere to be seen and I suffered an agonising drive fearing the rain would come down again and I felt defenceless without it. Never did I believe that a brand new riding mac costing umpteen pounds and 18 coupons would be returned to me. Half-heartedly, I reported it to the police station and I could hardly believe my eyes when I saw the policeman's wife running after me at the end of my round. "A gypsy boy brought it in", she said. "I told him to take it to the farm. I told him it belonged to the lady whose hair is turning grey. I didn't know your name." So delighted was I to know my mac was safe that it was some little time before the description of myself soaked in – there's a good deal to think about in that – "the lady whose hair is turning grey"!

However I have a nice compliment from Joe which I must relate to keep my end up. His wife asked him how I was getting on with my work and she told me he replied "Oh, Anne hasn't one lazy bone in her body".

1st October is the beginning of the farming year and assuredly there are great preparations and signs of winter. All day, loads of potatoes and mangles[36] are being brought in and stacked in the stables under straw. For weeks, old Jack and his son Sonny have been working on the corn ricks. Jack thatching and Sonny "pulling straw." They are a great contrast these two men – the slow going rheumaticky old father, with a sweet smile and very little conversation, and his son, a large limbed, fresh-faced brawny boy of 19, who is more good natured than anyone I have known and more simple-minded than I could have believed possible for modern days. He seems to combine the old age with the new. He works long and patiently, but with a skill and scientific outlook beyond that of the old "farmer's lad". When he is milking we are always half an hour earlier. He is expert with cows and horses, handling them with silence and sympathy. And yet he is mad keen to join the R.A.F. His dream is to "get cracking over Berlin". His eyes kindle when he talks of this and when aircraft pass overhead, he will stand in his white milking smock staring after them longingly.

The government refused to release him, so he has to be content with being a member of the N.F.S. He looks splendid in his uniform and prays 3 times a week for "a good old fire somewhere". I feel sorry when I see him "pulling straw" for thatching with his aged father. I feel his spirit of real adventure could be used to such advantage and yet I am glad, for I realise that it is his simplicity and knowledge of things fundamental that we shall need so vitally to build the post-war world.

I wish there were more "Sonny's" [sic], but perhaps there will be some day. He and Freda are getting very fond of each other and their shining faces betray what they probably regard as a hidden secret. I saw them this morning going to catch the horses across the frosty field with the sun shining on the white ground and on them. Freda's arm was around Sonny's shoulder (doubtless they felt they were alone in the world) – he in his smock and white milking cap, she in her khaki dungarees. It was a lovely scene and brought tears to my eyes. It was real HARDY.

"Only a maid and her wight whispering by

"War's annals will cloud into night, ere their story die"[37]

Another sign of winter is lamps in the cowshed when I arrive in the morning. It looks like a Christmas card with the moon and stars shining above and the cows silhouetted in heir stalls against the faint glow of a very old hurricane lamp.

And it is difficult to find the ponies – they are shrouded in half darkness and suspended layers of white mist. Often we search far for them and frequently get sidetracked by a forest pony which I mistake for Peter. The grass is losing its quality now, so a feed of oats is indicated for the ponies on their return from the round. They love it and Peter makes most delightful snorting noises in his nose when I take them to him. The cows also have to be "hayed down" each evening and every cow has a meal of cake and oats put ready in her stall for the afternoon milking. They come rushing in full speed now because of this and literally queue up along the lane, waiting for the gate to be opened. It is quite tricky because they are apt to eat up each other's rations and we have to be quick in chaining them up and seeing they are in their right stalls.

As a contrast to these signs of winter today, on this 28th day of October, I was given a large bowl of large and luscious raspberries (to eat with a slice of Swiss roll) picked from a customer's garden. And only a few days ago, a gypsy girl brought me a lovely bunch of primroses which she had gathered in the woods. In many gardens, when the sun is warm, I still see Red Admiral butterflies basking on Michaelmas daisy flowers.

One cottage garden was a picture, with a blaze of Michaelmas daisies, 4 or 5 Red Admirals, a giant yellow sunflower in the background.

Yesterday, I took a great bundle of straw for a dog who is returning from "Active Service." He has been away for a year and his owner will not be told how he has served his country till the war is over. She is preparing his kennel for him in order to give him a grand welcome.

I had a row with an old woman who is forever grumbling at her lack of milk. This week, as we were rather flush (3 cows have just calved), I thought I would stop her grumbles and give her extra. She obviously didn't want to afford it and after 2 or 3 days, said it had gone sour (impossible in this weather) and when yesterday she came to pay me, she refused the full price bellowing that I had never given her "full measure". She said she and her husband had measured it out all week and for a pint, I gave her ¾ and for a pint and a half, I gave only a pint with a teaspoonful over! For the sake of peace I deducted a few coppers and then said "If you give me your jug, I'll see what I have given you today." Rather fearfully, I poured the milk back into the measure and to my extreme relief, it filled it to the brim with about 3 drops to spare. I told the Boss and he said "Next time when there are 3 drops to spare, pour them back into the can and tell her that when she asks for a pint of beer she gets a pint with a thumb in it!!"

Accounts are always very delayed[38] and the poor NAAFI manager is forever in extremis to obtain his each week for stock-taking. Often months pass before he can eventually get hold of it. Joyce has been doing them, but when she is ploughing, everything else goes to the winds – and now she has left. So I have taken them over myself. The manager could hardly believe his eyes when I took [the account] into his office at the end of one week! He said, "That is really, very, very sweet of you my dear. I'll give you a piece of chocolate tomorrow." It tickled me no end to think of the wife of an Air Cdre "who is God Almighty of everything Airish in Palestine"[39] to be given a piece of chocolate for being a sweet girl!

Old George Wells,[40] the grandfather gypsy, has made me a lovely basket with New Park Farm straw from this harvest. It is so firm and strong and a nice, unusual round shape bound together with the bark of young saplings. I shall treasure it very much and feel kindly disposed towards him, although he is the ugliest looking man I've ever seen and most morose. For months I never bothered to speak to him, because any early pleasantries were ignored and so I thought he was deaf. I now discover he just pretends to be deaf when he doesn't want to hear!

November 1st to 14th

Another Fortnight on the Farm which passed very happily and all too quickly. It doesn't seem hard work at all after the milk round. In fact, I feel hardly exercised at the end of each day. Something unexpected always seems to crop up which relieves the monotony of any routine and of course Sundays are "red letter days" when I get home soon after 10 for a break till 1.30pm.

One day as I was just starting on the dairy, the Boss came in and said "Anne, will you go with Jack to fetch the things from Black Knoll?" Black Knoll is a large house which has just been sold and the "things" were two long stepladders, a wheelbarrow, 2 barrels, 2 chairs and a pig table, which the Boss had bought.

Gladly I went to the coach yard to help Jack harness Diana, the big carthorse. We took our huge hay wagon and set out across the open moor in the direction of Black Knoll. Oblivious of gorse, heather, small rivulets and ditches, we bumped along, Jack sitting by my side smoking peacefully while I drove. It was a lovely sunny morning with a slight dampness in the air which brought forth the smells of wet soil and rotting leaves and peat, and old Jack's tobacco mingled with them deliciously. He showed me rabbit burrows and foxes' holes and bushes of sloes and trees where nightingales had sung in the summer, and finally we reached "Black Knoll" and were welcomed into the stable yard by old "Mr Green," the gardener, a well-known figure to me, but one whom I had always regarded as rather forbidding. Today, I realised it was only his mask and behind that disapproving face hid a humorous teasing character.

He teased me about my milk float and then added seriously "As reg'lar as the clock you be, whenever I hears your pony trotting along that road, I knows it's near enough 12 o'clock." Then he chaffed old Jack about driving with nice land girls, which turned Jack quite pink, and I left the two old fellows to have a crack while I went to inspect the gardens.

It was fun getting our ladders etc. loaded onto the wagon and there was little room left for us when it was complete. We had a wander round the stables and the cowsheds and "Mr Green" told us how the old lady (the owner of the house) till after she was 80, was wont to come out and milk her special cow each morning at 7 o'clock, without fail.

With Jack sitting astride the wheelbarrow and myself perched on top of a barrel, we drove off once more and made a long detour home to find a way less bumpy than the moor with our unwieldy load. We followed a cart track round the edge of the forest, which made a pleasant drive, and I was interested to see a great tract of land which had been ploughed, and some for pasture, which was previously bog and heather and gorse. This is one of the Boss's enthusiasms – the cultivation of the New Forest. It is in its infancy as yet but holds

Anne records that the boss, Walter Gossling, was very much an advocate of ploughing up previously uncultivated land in the New Forest – often open land like this at Longslade Bottom. Food shortages meant a great need for more crops. There were opponents to this, but the war made it a necessity. Anne herself approved. Newly ploughed fields were also thought to be a deterrent to German planes landing. Some of the newly ploughed areas were so damp that they had to be ridge-and-furrowed, and even then were rather unproductive. Today such new-ploughed areas are still returning to natural land.
CREDIT: The Christopher Tower Reference Library, New Forest Centre, Lyndhurst

tremendous possibilities and this actual piece of land is the most successful they have dealt with. The Boss says one of the mistakes they have made was to be overruled by a few people who were against fences and enclosures and he says arable crops should be sown after the first ploughing as is the case with our newly ploughed land.

It was dinner time when Jack and I finally landed home and it was, as I said to the Boss, my idea of a really lovely morning's work.

Next day, I was told to help with the potatoes. We have a thousand sacks to fill for "Benbell" alone and only the sacks cost £50. We all sat on the wall of straw at the edge of the pit and selected good eaters to fill the sacks. Then we weighed them and sewed up the necks, a pleasant occupation and an undertaking so vast that it seemed impossible to try and hurry it up. The arrival of odd onlookers on their way to dinner induced a certain hilarity and soon we were all "shying" potatoes into the pit or throwing and catching to each other like schoolchildren. Benbell wanted 3 tons of potatoes by midday. Needless to say, he didn't get them and the Boss decided to hire a "gridder" which would do the job more quickly. It cost 10 shillings a day, but was certainly efficient. We just shovelled the potatoes in at one end, they passed over a grid which sorted the sizes, dropping the small and the medium potatoes, right and left in heaps on the ground, and sending the "eaters" up a caterpillar belt and then straight into a sack fixed at the end.

Pig from Anne's German trip sketchbook from 1926. Pigs featured in life at New Park, when, in the autumn, they were let out to forage freely for acorns and beech nuts. The ringing of a sow's nose is one of the diary's most dramatic episodes.

I was just about to help with this process next morning when I heard shouts and scuffles and saw an escaped sow careering with her 11 piglets through the farmyard. Jack and Joe were pig-ringing, putting rings through their noses to prevent them from burrowing into the ground. They hunt for grubs underneath the grass and make terrific holes all over the fields. This poor old sow had had one ring put in before she escaped, so she knew what she must avoid and simply refused to be caught. We chased her all round the farm, in and out of the stack yard, through the stables, up the drive, round the meadows, into the forest and back again, but we couldn't corner her. At last when it seemed desperate, and when none of us had any breath left, old Jack decided to try and lasso her. Twice he got the noose round her head, but twice she turned and escaped. Then he put the noose at the end of a long pole, but again she double-crossed him. The last time, she plunged madly under a barbed wire fence and Sonny got hold of her tail and held hard, yelling for us to help. Old Joe caught her left leg and I got her right one and Jack flung the rope into her open mouth and around her nose. It was a neat bit of work and she was powerless. We got her fettered to a post while Jack put 3 more rings into her nose while she sobbed and wailed at the top of her voice – a most human and upsetting sound. The four men were as emotionally wrought up as I was and stood in grim silence with set, unhappy faces. The 11 little piglets remained oblivious to this sad drama – they frisked and fought and frolicked in the sunshine whilst their poor mother sobbed her heart out.

A new land girl arrived today and our speculations as to what she might be like led Eileen to confide in me and describe the uproar provoked by my arrival.

Apparently, when I arrived for my interview, the farmer's wife refused to have me at any price – aided and abetted by Dorothy. "They set to and made an awful scene" and screamed that nothing would induce them to consider me. The poor Boss, knowing I was sitting in the next door room and could probably hear the uproar (I didn't!) implored them to be quiet. At last, when I departed, he went in and said "Well anyway, she's gone and she probably won't come back" so they quietened down for a day or so till my letter arrived saying that I would "start work on Tuesday!" "There's a letter from her and she's coming!" yelled Mrs G, almost in a state of apoplexy. "I tell you, I won't have any Air Force officer's wives here," she screamed, whereupon they all formed a sort of trades union whereby they'd give me such Hell I wouldn't be able to stick it for more than a week. Even old Joe refused to speak to me. They were going to give me all the beastly jobs to do and all the cows-that-kick to milk and that would be the end of that! But what I'm sure they didn't know was that the Boss had written to me and said he hoped I should find my "work and my surroundings very agreeable" and that I felt a response in him that made up for all their surliness. No wonder I found that first week a bit tough! Never shall I forget it. It was uphill work indeed, but I think I may truly say that they are all now my friends. The very fact that they can now be so amused at their reaction then proves it. Eileen said to Dorothy today "Now don't say a word about the new girl – remember what you said about Anne".

The new girl is a Lancashire lass with the strong accent and the vigorous actions of the Northerner. She is 17 and entirely self possessed and I should say very efficient, but I also must reserve my opinions till a later date.

News came that mother was ill. When could I go to Scotland? I was on the round and Eileen was on leave, so there was just no-one to take my place. What a dilemma! Was mother really ill enough to justify my leaving the farm in a jam? Yet, if I didn't go now, would I be too late? What should I do? Wires passed from England to Scotland and back again, crossing each other most unsatisfactorily and still I hung on, with the Boss's guarantee that I should go North at a minute's notice if necessary. "Meanwhile," he said "teach Olive[41] the round and she can take over as soon as she has learnt it."

For four days I took Olive with me. The first day was fun. She was still new and strange and I did a bit of showmanship and enjoyed being the old hand. It was pleasant to find how really experienced I was at the job and most satisfying to find that it puzzled her now as much as it had puzzled me 6 months ago. Then followed three days of agony, when I let Olive take over the reins (literally) and I just sat and watched. Impatient young vixen! What had been a pleasure to me now became just a series of aggravating incidents. Poor Peter was harried and whipped, his head tugged and curses shouted if for a moment he slackened his speed.

In vain, I tried to encourage that he should be driven as an individual and not as a machine, but to no avail. "This damn HORSE," she would grumble, "I can't be bothered with him at all". And I gave up the unequal struggle, but inwardly I raged and longed for the day when I could have Peter to myself again. My nice elderly customers were just "bothersome old fools" to Olive and if the can refused to open in a second, she would kick it and swear loud Lancashire curses and then go stomping off in a fury. Nothing could hurry her, in spite of her impatience, and each day we got back later and later till I felt I could bear it no longer. "They'll just have to wait," said Olive – and they had to! We would arrive home to find the farm champing with wrath and I would rush through the bottle washing in apoplectic speed, while Olive calmly took her "hour off for lunch" and sallied forth at 4.30 to feed round a wisp of hay to the cows.

At last those four unhappy days were ended and on the fifth day I set out for Scotland, not caring how long it took, very content to sit back in my corner seat or even on the floor of the refreshment room, as I had to at Preston, where I was flung out in the middle of the night and called for next morning. It was blissful to have just nothing to do and no companion to jar my senses. Travelling in wartime is a lengthy procedure, especially near Christmas and this journey took me exactly 24 hours instead of 12. But I felt not the least fussed or infuriated. Have I so soon acquired the philosophy of the farmer?

When daylight came, I eagerly looked from my window to find rolling hillsides and stone walls. How familiar they seemed. And how orderly were the neat grey farmsteads. This whole countryside seemed more tidy and more methodical than the one I had left, and very lovely, quite as lovely as the lush meadowlands of Hampshire, but I refused to compare them. They are both part of myself and I love them both.

My visit was unexpectedly a happy one. Mother was already well on the road to recovery and in excellent spirits. A domestic crisis which caused me to "bed and feed" at the local inn suited me admirably, for here I was free to come and go as I chose, to go to bed when I felt sleepy and to rise when I felt inclined. Also this very week, there was a large sale of pedigree cattle and the Inn was full, indeed overflowing, with farmers from every part of Scotland and some from Yorkshire. Here was my chance at last to discuss the many farming problems I had been puzzling about. At every meal, I was squeezed in at a different table, between handsome young farmers and lonely old side-whiskered ones, who wore tweed hats and shiny stiff collars. They too were eager for information. The wartime policy of agriculture in England? The cultivation of the New Forest? Ley grazing?[42] Etc and I answered to the best of my ability, feeling very knowledgeable when I could give a satisfactory reply. I was really pleased with myself one day, I remember, till an old farmer suddenly asked "What acreage is your farm?" and roared with laughter when I haltingly admitted I didn't know. I have since found it is 600 acres.[43]

It was frosty in Scotland, with a round full moon shining in a cloudless sky night after night. One evening, I walked beside the loch[44] and saw it reflected in the water with the white hills and bare trees mirrored as clear as day. There was no sound, not a ripple of the water, and I stood silent, breathing that cold night air, watching the moon rise almost visibly into the great domed sky. How lovely it was. A grand memory to bring back to England, which I can see still and when I visualise it, I can again feel that icy air which was so thin and clear against my cheeks.

As I travelled southwards, the weather changed and although Hampshire had been frosty in my absence, it greeted my return with blue skies and balmy sunshine. Incredibly it was Christmas week, although it seemed more like spring. But despite the weather, the Christmas spirit was rampant and it was an exciting, full week. Spirits ran high. Everyone in the gayest of moods planned for the Christmas weekend – how we would stagger our time off and what we should do with it. There was much to be done in preparation for those three days and we were grateful for the fine weather in which to do it all. The main items were to get an immense supply of wood for the fires and enough hay to fill all of the three barns for the cows, calves, horses and ponies. The gypsies dealt with the wood, bringing back great loads from the forest and I went hay-carting with Sonny and hay-carting with Jack. Both were delightful experiences and each so different.

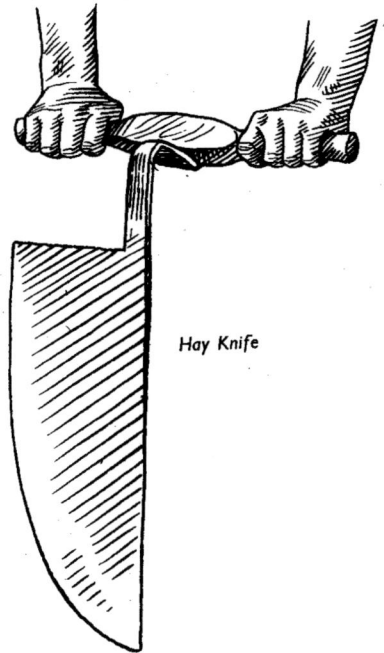

Hay Knife

A hay-knife, wrote Derek H. Chapman in his *A Farm Dictionary*, published in 1952, is "a knife with a very large blade and a handle sticking out at right angles at one end, used for slicing bales of hay out of the stack." Anne described her difficulty in using this tool: "Sonny taught me to cut chunks of hay out of the rick, with a great hay knife – 'the Home Guard spike' as he calls it. It looked so easy in his hands and so clumsy in mine..." (Illustration by Evelyn Dunbar)

Pitchfork

Pitching hay up onto a wagon requires skill. Evelyn Dunbar, in *A Book of Farmcraft*, draws a pitchfork so that a novice knows precisely how to wield it.

With Sonny, work was vigorous, noisy and gay. We chattered and laughed and made jokes and whistled carols and sang songs. Sonny taught me to cut chunks of hay out of the rick, with a great hay knife – "the Home Guard spike" as he calls it.

It looked so easy in his hands and so clumsy in mine and I would puff and pant as I tried to plunge it into the rick, till Sonny would laughingly wrest it from me and in a second I would hear the clear crunch of cut stalks and a lovely neat square would fall out, ready to be thrown on the wagon. He would pitch whilst I would load – an art I had not appreciated before, which is most skilled.

A wagon is loaded from the sides to the middle and loaded in layers so that it can be easily and quickly unloaded in the same layers. The sides must be built up square to make a good sized load and solid so that the top will not swing off. The man who loads must needs ride back on top of the hay, as it is too high for him to jump off and a most adventurous ride it is across the bumpy fields, where the old wagon rolls and sways, and along the muddy lane where one must bury one's head in the hay to escape the branches which hang low enough to scrape the surface. I loved those rides on those mild, sunshiny days when one could relax so unexpectedly and lie smelling the sweet hay as if it were summertime again and let my body roll in rhythm with the wagon and feel so near the sky that aeroplanes overhead seemed very low. I got a surprisingly different perspective from this height, almost a bird's eye view of the fields and hedges and the lovely old Farmstead couched among the trees and cows grazing, red and white blobs on the green, and the old horse Diana jogging along, whose broad back was almost all I could see of her.

With Jack, hay-carting was a silent, tranquil occupation. We loaded only as much as we had time for, quietly and steadily, and as we worked our thoughts would wander on and only occasionally would we break the silences. It was as peaceful and harmonious as work with Sonny was gay, but I liked when we were loaded up to watch old Jack lighting up his pipe and to smell his tobacco smoke rising to me among the hay and then to jog our way homewards in time to knock off for lunch.

WRONG

RIGHT

WRONG

RIGHT

LOADING A CART

Back to basics. Dunbar's illustrations showing the right and the wrong way to do things, like loading a cart, are practical and also entertaining.

Three days before Christmas, a rushed order came for potatoes and Eileen and I were sent down to the kennels to bag them up. This suited us down to the ground because we were both anxious to do a little last minute shopping and the kennels are on the way to the village. We decided we must work quickly and get to Brockenhurst in the lunch hour. Full of zeal, we cycled down to the kennels with our piles of sacks. Potatoes piled up on the roof were covered with straw. We uncovered them with speed and dragged out the scales. "Goodness!" cried Eileen, "however many pounds are there in a hundredweight?" Neither of us had any idea. We had quite forgotten. We were absolutely floored and then all of a sudden Eileen was inspired "112lbs, 1 cwt" she said firmly. We worked like niggers and got to the village in time for our shoppings and a Christmas noggin and cycled farmwards feeling exceedingly hilarious and very noisy.

Christmas Eve

At long last, Christmas Eve had arrived – a glorious white day with hot sun and a blue sky. Would it be like this tomorrow? All preparations now complete, we had time to stand about and gossip. The gypsies kept walking through the farmyard with bunches of mistletoe "for sale" and Sonny returned from the forest carrying a great armful of holly, red with berries, and bits stuck at a rakish angle in his black beret. He looked magnificent in his green coat and his red round face –

"and his face was as round as red and as round as a berry."[45]

We were all impatient to be off now, so with many shouts of "A Merry Christmas" we jumped onto our cycles for home. I noticed a thaw had set in. Rain, I feared, and I was right.

Christmas Day

Christmas Day dawned damp and muggy – very disappointing, but the weather was soon forgotten in the excitement of Christmas morning. While it was still dark we arrived each loaded with gifts and, by the light of lanterns, and with much hilarity, we exchanged our presents and there was indeed a spirit of "peace and goodwill" on our cowsheds.

We did the minimum amount of work and with such willing co-operation that we hardly noticed it. I had Christmas Day and Sunday "half days" off and on Boxing Day, I did the milk round and received gifts of eggs and honey (in sections) and cakes and cigarettes from customers who were kind enough to be grateful for my services. The round could have become an orgy of Christmas drinks, but eager not to tarry, I resisted all except a neat whisky provided by the wife of the taxi driver. Eileen was a sport and worked backwards on my round when she had finished hers, till we met and together we drove home in our two floats like two charioteers, along a strangely empty road.

Christmas has come and gone and now I can look forward to the spring. The shortest day is already passed and now we are beginning to climb out of the dark pit of winter, which I confess now I had dreaded. How quickly it has gone and I actually enjoyed it, perhaps more even than those hot, long summer days when I longed to lie and laze and soak in gorgeous sunshine when every movement was an effort. I loved winter with its lamps and crackling fires and crispy mornings, when I did my work with a sort of outside energy. And every day at dawn, I experienced that most wonderful sensation, when daylight came, when suddenly it would seem as if a weight were lifted from my shoulders, when I could raise my head and lift my eyes and see. I enjoyed the frosty days and snowy days when the ponies were rough shod, milk frozen in the pail and roads slippery. Then the round was really an adventure – and adventures are always exhilarating!

January 1944

The Beginning of a New Year

"Of all the months, January most persistently looks both ways. The frosts strengthen as the days lengthen, but in almost every year it smells of spring" (The Countryman)[46]

January 16th

January this year has indeed lived up to her reputation of frosty days and balmy days intermixed and I think the balmy days have predominated, when the sun shone out of a clear blue sky hour after hour, when one could sit in a sheltered corner and take off one's coat and feel the warmth soaking through and marvel at such strength of heat so early. One's whole being seems to relax and expand and a great joy surges up inside exclaiming "Spring is here!"

Tiny buds are appearing everywhere. Primrose and foxglove plants are already green in the hedges and in the gardens, patches are purple with sweet violets. One yellow crocus has appeared and one willow tree curves like a fountain of green water towards the stream. Snowdrops are everywhere and catkins, shiny and soft and grey are so familiar it seems but a short time since we saw them.

January 22

Promotion

It is the Sunday ritual at the farm each week to seize old Joe's Sunday papers and to read our horoscope! Whether it was due to my horoscope "Archimedes" which said "An exciting week, a big surprise" or just the spring feeling in my bones, I do not know. But anyway, I felt excited and gay and carefree and I did the round in grand style, rushing from house to house, eating hot waffles at the Canadian Mess and a slice of chocolate log "left by Monty" at the General's headquarters! Saturday came and I remembered my horoscope. "No surprise", I thought, but I spoke too soon. Nearly at my last house when I was stooping to take some empty bottles from a newspaper on the doorstep and putting my full bottle in its place, I suddenly saw Mac's face beaming up at me in the most unexpected way. I stared and stared again. There he was and there, below, I read the magic letters – A.V.M.[47] What joy and excitement. I had a gin there and then, round or no round, and sped back to tell the good news. There was great delight and the Boss seemed almost to share my pride. He beamed for days. News spread like wildfire round the village and many strange remarks were made to Olive who took my place on the round next day. Several people asked her if I were "a Lady" and one old woman said "She comes from Lunnon and there's a photograph of her husband in the newspaper. I'll show it to you" – whereupon she produced a large scale photograph of General Eisenhower!

I sent off cables and received letters of congratulations and finally had news that Mac was transferred from Palestine to Middle East, so now I keep a bag packed in case he suddenly comes on leave.

However, there was little time for daydreaming, for suddenly everyone (except myself) got ill. One after another, they went down with flu or gastritis or poisoned fingers or some strange complaint or other. It meant very hard work and no days off for ages for those who were left and one whole week when Joe was away, I reached the farm by 5.30 in time to get the cows in. Long days I spent cutting cabbages, cutting kale and carting hay. Meanwhile, the spring advanced and beech buds gleamed brown against the sky and daffodils swung gaily in the grass.

March 20

Sowing Oats

All this time, we have been shorthanded and working like Trojans. "This is the busiest time of all", the Boss says. "What we can sow now depends what we can reap later." And he has ricked his shoulder and can do very little. With his usual wonderful patience, he says nothing, but he looks miserable. However today he said he'd like me to go down to the park with him to help him with the Drill, to sow oats. I was thrilled. For days and days while Dorothy has been ill I have had charge of the calves entirely – 33 of them all on different diets – and if there is one animal I really hate it is a calf. Or rather I should say calves. One is manageable, but more than one are quite impossible to deal with. Joe agrees with me that they just cannot be controlled. It is useless to talk to them or shout at them. You can't say "gere ba-ack" as you can to a horse or "away" as you can to a dog. They just take not the least heed. They come at you full force and buffet you and bump you from all sides and stamp their hooves on your foot and plunge their heads in your bucket so greedy are they for their food. Sometimes when I see red, I whack them with my hand, but they feel nothing and it hurts me till I could weep with anger and frustration. Feeding calves is the only time when I really lose my temper and later, when I see them lying peacefully chewing their cud, watching the world with eyes of baby wonderment, I reprove myself fiercely and wonder how I could ever be so brutal.

So today, I left them joyfully for Dorothy and drove off to the park feeling rather as if we were going for a jaunt. I had not been to the Park since October and it was good to see it again still looking beautiful with bare trees and furrowed land. The winter wheat was already showing green, a glorious vivid green, bright in the sunshine. This was one of our most spring-like days. No wind, hot sun and a blue sky. I worked in a cotton shirt with my sleeves rolled up and still I was hot. My job was to sit behind on the drill and work the gears while the Boss drove the tractor. I had also to watch that the seed came properly down and into the drills. It was very bumpy on the rough ground but every so often I had a rest when we came to a sack of seed and filled up the box.

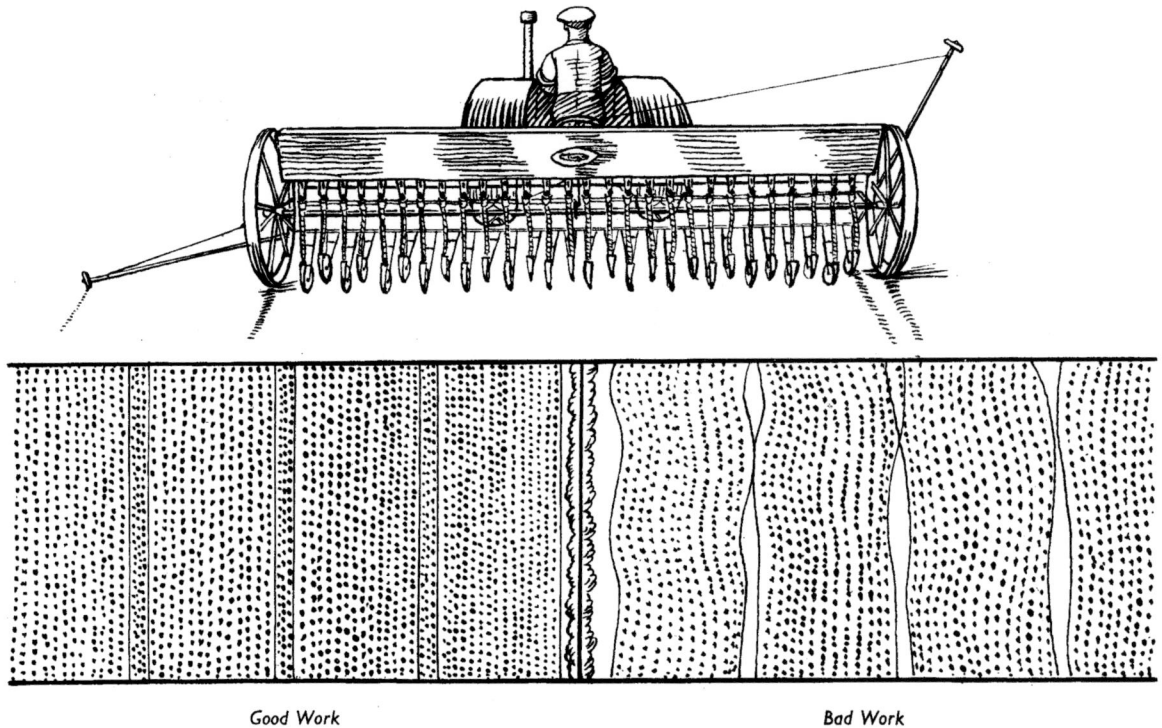

Good Work   *Bad Work*

CORN-DRILL

A corn-drill was used to sow wheat, oats, barley, peas, beans – and of course corn – by making shallow furrows, into which the seed is sown. Dunbar's *A Book of Farmcraft* diagram shows the need to avoid "undrilled spaces." Anne records her participation: "My job was to sit behind on the drill and work the gears while the boss drove the tractor. I had also to watch that the seed came properly down..."

I did enjoy it working peacefully up and down the great 30-acre field, the highest point of ground for miles around, the Boss's familiar figure in front of me and old "Bray" trotting behind with a smile on his face of utter contentment and his four feet planted always in the narrow rut made by the wheel of the drill. If ever we stopped, he would bark madly and rush round in circles till we started again, for to him, a stoppage meant Something Wrong!

And so we worked on hour after hour in perfect harmony, with the sun blazing down and an occasional aircraft whirring overhead. Once, when we had been filling up with seed and the Boss was just about to start up again, he turned round and said to me "And to think that you could be sat in an armchair in this glorious sunshine if you wanted to!" And I replied, "I'd much rather be doing this though." And he said "So would I!" Yes indeed, I was thrilled to be sowing grain for this year's harvest and knew what a maternal pride I should take in it when it began to grow. We have had a long drought, weeks and weeks with never a drop of rain. We need it badly and I longed for it for my oats.

Before today, I had hated tractors. Nasty, noisy, smelly things I thought them. I should try not to learn to drive them. I'd rather stay peacefully driving Peter or milking cows. But today, somehow, the tractor became alive. She seemed to purr over the ground and I saw her with new eyes; an animate thing doing a job of work patiently and willingly. And yes, she was even beautiful. With her dull green paint and rusty chimneys contrasted with the brown earth and bare trees. Before I had fully weighed the consequences, I blurted out "Please may I drive her for a little?" And there I was, half an hour later, firmly in her toils, fascinated as she led me up and down and back again, over the rough soil. I knew I was lost – mesmerized. I should never be really happy till I could drive her – by myself. Just herself and me in the wide bare field working together. That was my desire. But I told no-one. I was so afraid of being disappointed, I just waited and prayed that one day it should happen.

At 5 o'clock, the Boss stopped and, looking at the sky ruefully, said "Well we'd better knock off for tea now, I suppose?" "I'm game to go on if you are", I said, knowing it was my tea and not his own he was thinking of. A smile of great content spread over his face and so once more we started up, now edging the field four times, each time round a mile and a quarter long, but we finished just about 7 o'clock and it was still light, though the air was chilly now and the sun low. How wonderful these long evenings are. I had almost regretted their coming, when I could no longer dig myself in by my fire with curtains drawn and candles flickering, isolated and alone with my thoughts and my books. But now they are here, I love them and delight as each day lengthens. Tonight I was as hungry as a hunter and greedily devoured a whole breast of cold chicken and salad, with cider to drink. The chicken was given to me by Jack, who had "kept it specially" for me, and how tender it was. It is the first chicken I have ever eaten all by myself.

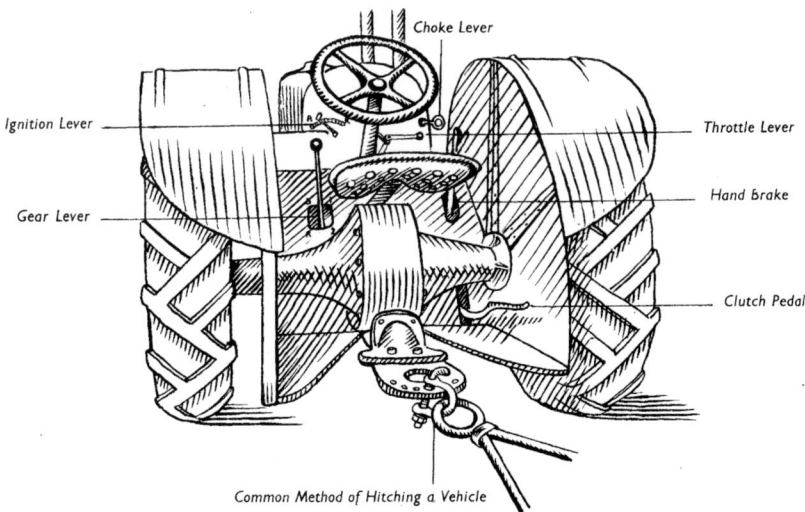

Ignition Lever
Gear Lever
Choke Lever
Throttle Lever
Hand Brake
Clutch Pedal
Common Method of Hitching a Vehicle

Anne's fascination with tractors grows. She starts by pretending the last thing she wants to do is drive one but quietly takes the opportunity when it occurs. Then she soon admits she has become "wedded" to the machine.
(Illustration by Evelyn Dunbar).

March 31st

Distributing Fertiliser

Eleven whole days later and I was still dreaming about that tractor, when Dorothy rushed into the cowshed and shouted "You and me for the Park today Anne. We've got to work on the distributor." My heart leapt. But what exactly did this mean? All the time I had been there, Dorothy had never touched the tractor. I knew she could drive it, but I gathered she didn't like it and if Dorothy doesn't like a thing, being the daughter-of-the-house, she just doesn't do it. Would she, I wondered, like it better now? Sonny was on the sick list. The fertiliser had first poisoned his face and now it had attacked his feet. He has terribly delicate skin, an astonishing weakness for such a brawny youth, and now he was hobbling about with bandaged feet doing nothing. This surely was my chance? If Dorothy could be got rid of! I would show no enthusiasm and I would pretend tractor-driving was the thing I hated most. So I sat on the mudguard wearily, while Dorothy held my beloved wheel and we climbed up and down the steep hillside sprinkling white fertiliser wherever we went. What beastly stuff it was. A strong wind was blowing, which blew it all over us. Our hair was soon like powdered wigs. It blew into our eyes, making them smart, down our throats, making them dry and got into every cut and crack in our hands till they smarted and burnt. Sacks were placed all over the field and these had to be tipped into the distributor at intervals. Great heavy sacks which we could scarcely lift. The Boss was to come down when it was time to stop, but he forgot we had had no lunch and left us there till 4.15pm. Hungrier and hungrier we grew and I soon saw that Dorothy was wearying. When I was quite sure, I said magnanimously "Shall I take her for a bit now?" and changed places with Dorothy in a casual manner. Dorothy was obviously more happy lying on the mudguard, so there she stayed and I was still driving in a nonchalant manner when the Boss arrived. Nothing was said, but I saw him see, and back we went for lunch, tea and supper all rolled into one. Actually, I was too tired and over hungry to have much appetite. I felt whacked, but I felt that things were moving in the right direction.

April 5th

Ploughing

"Will you come with me to Long Meadow this morning Anne? I'd like to get you going on the tractor", said the Boss, when I came in after the milking. "Certainly, I'll ask Freda to hay round", I said "then I can be there sooner".

Freda was in the dairy cleaning up. "You've got to hay round", I told her, "I'm working on the tractor in Long Meadow and if I'm not back by tea time, you'd better do the calves". I rushed out before she could see my grin of triumph. I had no intention of being back in time to do the calves. I was going to drive the tractor all day!

When we reached Long Meadow, there was the plough waiting for us. We oiled it and greased it and attached it to the tractor and set off. Long Meadow is a long strip of ground, cleared out of the forest, fully a quarter of a mile long, the Boss says. A triangle was already ploughed in one corner to even up the edges and a few furrows right down the centre from end to end. We started off, with one wheel of the tractor moving along the last rut and the plough turning over two furrows behind, making a deep, well-defined line at the edge. I had to keep a constant watch on the wheel of the tractor in front and the wheel of the plough behind to keep them perfectly in line with the previous furrow. It was fascinating to look back and see the blades rolling over great sods of turf and turning grass, dandelions and daisies out of sight. The sharp knives polished the surface of the soil, so that it shone in the sunlight. I have read that good ploughing should be very shiny and each side the same height like the roof of a house. When I came to the end of each row, I had to turn the tractor sharply round the top and at the same moment pull a rope attached to the gear behind, on the plough, to lift up the blades and then again at the beginning of the new row get the tractor into position and immediately drop the blades – quite a tricky procedure. The first time I "muffed it" and grew very pink. The Boss was riding on the tractor behind me and when I was due for another "lift", I noticed he jumped off and busied himself with the fence, looking the other way. I did it beautifully that time and was indeed grateful for his tact.

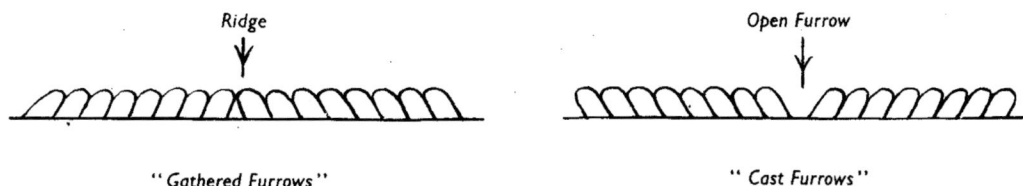

Anne, who was absorbed by the art of ploughing, would have appreciated Dunbar's diagram of "cast" and "gathered" furrows from *A Farm Dictionary*.

Presently, he went away and I realised my dream had at last come true. Here I was alone with my tractor, ploughing up a piece of Mac's England. I looked and saw the green strips getting thinner as I added furrow after furrow to the brown rectangle. I stood up very straight and the tractor purred on tirelessly until the Boss came to relieve me for my lunch hour. I had brought sandwiches down with me, so I saw at the edge of the wood to eat them and have a smoke while the Boss took over. When I rejoined him, feeling refreshed, he said "Are you ready for another go, or would you like to pick primroses? There are plenty in the wood." That is the sort of kindliness and consideration he shows, which makes me feel I'd work my inside out for him! I did pick primroses beside a tiny stream and wood anemones – a lovely interlude – and then back to the plough again till 6 o'clock. There was now left only a narrow strip of green 2 or 3 feet wide along the hedge – the rest I had turned into a billowing sea of brown and shiny waves. Have I ever felt so proud? But I felt exhausted also, with excitement and fatigue. It is a heavy job and my shoulders and arms ached.

Freda and Sonny wandered down to fetch me. "Sorry I couldn't get back to do the calves", I said to her. "But I had to finish this" I added, waving my arms airily across the meadow.

April 16th

Wedded to Elizabeth

That thrilling, exciting period of courtship is over. Elizabeth and I have been together for one whole week and our romance has resolved itself into something infinitely deep and wonderful. I have come to know her and sense her every mood. Every sound and movement betrays her inner emotions and with the intuition of true love, I find myself dealing with her instinctively. How wonderful life can be when we are together and alone, in the wide open spaces. When she sings to me, her voice is sweeter than the nightingale – and oh how I dread the day when her song shall cease.

The land we ploughed together, we have "disced"[48] twice, rolled, sown and rolled again. The Boss took her over for the sowing and I worked the gears on the drill. His presence did not jar, for we were all in tune on that glorious April day with sunshine and blue sky and white clouds. At the request of the War Agricultural Committee, we have sown Long Meadow for experimental purposes, so it will be interesting to see what results we get. Another experiment we have tried for ourselves is sowing grass seed together with oats, instead of oats first, followed by grass. The grass usually is sown afterwards on a field which we want to grass down for next year, after we have reaped the oats.

One afternoon, the Boss borrowed Elizabeth for discing "Lower Hollands Wood Field" and told me to follow after with the large tractor and the tandem-roller. He was about quarter of a field ahead of me, but my tractor was faster, so I soon began to catch him up and it was fun watching the distance between us getting less and less and purring up and down the long rows, sometimes meeting, sometimes passing each other, like a tramp steamer and a little yacht. There was too much noise to shout greetings but we waved and grinned and each proceeded on our course.

The tandem roller is an immense affair with one central roller and one at each side, altogether covering about 40 feet of ground at once. It is ridged like an oatcake rolling pin and I love to look behind and see the shaded effect of dozens of thin links marked on the soil in contrast to the rough knobbly ground which has just been disced. Once when I was in full swing down the centre of the field, I heard a click – the pin attaching the roller to the tractor had slipped out, leaving the roller motionless and sending me shooting away about 20 yards at the rate of knots.

Today Elizabeth and I have been ploughing the "Kennel Field" for potatoes, a nice flat field of about 22 acres. The only drawback being a small pond at one end which I feared I might be mesmerized into. I took great pride in my furrows and was pleased with them. Ploughing is the most fascinating of all field work, especially when great clouds of black crows follow behind. There have been no seagulls this year, although we are so near the coast. I suspect that they are content with what they find in the English Channel.

This is the end of my month on the farm and tomorrow I set off on the milk round again. I have deep regrets, but Elizabeth has promised to be faithful to me and Peter will give me a consolation. The Boss, knowing how much I hate Peter to be driven by Olive (who has no sympathy for ponies), ordered him to be put out to grass when I came off the round and I am to have him tomorrow. Of course no reason was given, but I know why! Every day, I have a chat with him and give him a head of kale or a handful of oats and bring him into the stable for the night.

One evening when I was late getting back, no-one could catch him and when I came along, they stood in a crowd in the yard to see what I could do. I climbed under the fence, called "Come along Peter boy!" and Peter, a tiny black speck in the remote distance of the field, lifted his head and walked towards me and when quite near, broke into a trot! When I was leading him round to the stable, the Boss came out grinning and said "We'll have to call you Bronco Busto!" Another night when I was late and went straight home, and I admit forgot Peter in my desire for food, nobody could catch him and he had to stay out all night. Yes Peter will certainly give me consolation. I sometimes even wonder if it may be I who shall be unfaithful, once I get out on the road again?

Elizabeth's real name is Lizzie – being one of the well-known Fordsons. (But I prefer to think of her as Elizabeth.)[49]

Monday April 17

Back on the Round

I had the greatest surprise when I sallied forth onto the roads again. I emerged into an inferno of din and traffic and suddenly realised that for a whole month I had been apart from the world altogether. Just cycling across the moor to and from the farm, I had seen nothing of the speed up in our preparations for the invasion of the continent. Now I found myself in a swirl of traffic and troops. Huge tanks, great armoured vehicles and "Ducks"[50] and invasion craft of every description was being whirled along the roads in frantic speed. It seemed grim and terrific after my peaceful fields. I had lost my traffic sense and felt that everything was coming at me. I was astonished at Peter's cool reaction, but then it was not new to him. That first day was a nightmare. To add to my discomfort, I was driving a huge farm cart because I was in the throes of painting my little float and it needed several evenings to complete. This cart was so high, with no step, that I had to attach a loop of rope to pull myself up and it was exceedingly exhausting.

To add to the general confusion, roads were being widened all along my route. What a din! Grinding convoys of tanks added to great drills working on the tarmac. My head reeled. However could I stand this for a month? I thought with longing of the peaceful bare fields and Elizabeth humming rhythmically but, as they say, one gets accustomed to everything and after a day or so, I felt as calm as Peter. I took out my little float on the third day, painted a bright yellow, with green lettering "W. H. Gossling – New Park Farm – Direct from the Farm" in green lettering. It did look clean and gay and I felt inordinately proud of it. I had washed and mended Peter's little yellow ear caps and made green tassels for the tips to replace the old blue ones. He looked lovely with his shiny black coat and crimpy mane floating out in the breeze. Everyone noticed my float and smiled indulgently. And the soldiers, many of them from the north, were vastly amused at Peter's ear caps. They shouted "What are they for? Has he got earache?" "Are they to keep his nose from running?" etc. but when I answered that they were to keep the flies away, they sobered and realised they were functional and not merely decorative. One soldier stood in my way and stopped me, saying "Milkmaid, you're the very person I wanted to see". He then held out his hand, showing a huge wart on the back, and explained he had been told the only thing that would cure it was to tie round a horse's hair. Could I get him one? "Pull one out of Peter's tail" I said, which he did, and departed very gleefully.

I had a most triumphant passage through the village, everyone admiring my "new float" and gasping incredulously when I said I painted it myself. Somebody likened me to Phoebus, driving in my sun chariot, which was quite a change from being a Boadicea! I laughed when mother wrote and told me to buy a green and yellow frock (at her expense) to go with it. I could see myself in a straw hat, wreathed with buttercups, not quite the correct kit for a Land Girl.

And so the days went on. I had a whole month of glorious unceasing sunshine, when I watched spring turn almost to summer. Dawn had arrived when I wakened at 5.30am to the tumultuous sound of birdsong. And they were still exulting in their matins as I crossed the moor, dew laden and misty. On April 22nd, the first cuckoo sang and that I felt was the first real sign of summer.

The spring bulbs gave place to flowering currant, deep and pale lilacs wisteria and orange blossom, all filling the air with scent. Wallflowers, polyanthus and great crimson peonies massed the flower beds with colour and everywhere I was given great bunches of flowers to take home. Lettuces and rhubarb too, which I ate with relish, as I gleefully changed my hot meal at night into a cold salady one. Life has become so simplified with no fires and less cooking and there is a feeling of great relaxation in the evenings, with windows wide open and no black-out and my rooms a bower full of flowers. The children at the farm pick me bunches of orchids and bluebells and I stick them into any available pot in their tight little bunches. They look so gay and the gypsies bring me large quantities of watercress straight from the forest streams – a very different proposition from the watercress one buys in shops which has lost its crispness and its flavour.

One very hot day, when the sun blazed down on the main road, I drove back by "the cover" – a winding track through the forest to the farm, which is impassable in winter. It was cool and beautiful beneath the trees, beeches a fresh, lovely green, bushes of May blossom coming into flower and bluebells carpeting the ground.

As I skirted the edge of "Lower Hollands Wood" field, I could scarcely believe my eyes. There it stretched away on my right no longer brown and bare, but the softest, most subtle green o'erspread it. It was my wheat. Hundreds and thousands of tiny blades rose through the soil, so tender that they gave the appearance of a soft bloom. I experienced a feeling of gratitude and great contentment. I stopped Peter, lit up a cigarette and wandered slowly home – rather thoughtful.

The troops have changed at a certain Mess where I take milk. They have been replaced by 50-50 British-Americans. The first few days were complete havoc. I take my milk into a big kitchen which serves over a hundred officers. Apparently the British officers like dishes cooked one way and the Americans another, the one like tea and the other like coffee, one potatoes boiled and the other fried. And the poor cooks (who are British) didn't know whether they were on their head or their heels. The British breakfast is good, honest-to-God porridge and bacon and friend egg. The American, a queer, thick cereal like sago[51] which is served in lumps and what they call "flap jacks" to follow, being hot pancakes, with melted

This rare photo of black American GIs in The New Forest was taken by Stan Orchard. Canadian and American, as well as British troops flooded the New Forest in preparation for D-Day - the Allied invasion of Normandy. The build-up is a backdrop to Anne's diary, reminding today's readers of those nightmarish, fraught times. The arrival of American GIs, "talking big," instigated a variety of cultural challenges. Though the Americans were renowned for generosity, and the Canadian soldiers gave the local children unforgettable Christmas and New Year parties, there could sometimes be friction between the troops and the locals. But there was also much friendship. Richard Taylor's 1995 book, *Before We Go, Brockenhurst Memories of Peace and War* includes a quote from a "real tough old forester. The old man said, 'The Americans seem very decent, but those white ones they have brought along, I don't like them.' He found that the black Americans were at heart countrymen, who knew about forest ways and how to live in the countryside." The names of everyone in this photo are known: from left to right: Robert Watkins (GI), Trainer Burdon, Albert William (GI), Roy Read, Buck Northington (GI) and Evit Gulliver. The picture was taken on July 6 1944, a month after D-Day. These G.I.s would probably be in Brockenhurst with 611 Quartermaster Battalion.

syrup and rashers of bacon on top. They gave me a plateful of this and my word, it was good. I cook it now for my own supper, substituting fried bread for pancakes which are too much of a palaver for me to mix. There was a feeling of great restraint when they first arrived. The kitchen staff stood in isolated groups metaphorically speaking, miles apart. The British on one side and the Americans at the other side of an unseen barrier, but each day the tension gradually grew less and after a week or so, they were all mingled and joking together in grand style – a real Anglo-American Alliance! One English soldier I spoke to said what a good thing it was. (He came from Manchester and visited our farm because he had never "seen milk coming out of a cow.") He told me that when they were segregated and met in a pub, there was always a fight, but "now we are working together we understand each other and get along fine". He said, "You know, they're just like overgrown schoolboys. They don't mean to brag, they just talk big!"

Another soldier, a Welshman, asked me where he could buy a 'laying hen' to send to his wife – she lives in Wales and has already three, but is too shy to buy another herself. So I got one from Joe and cycled down with it one evening in my bicycle box. There was great joy when I carried it in my arms into the kitchen and roars of laughter when I told them its name was Violet (it wasn't but I thought it would sound good). This appealed specially to the Americans. I told the man who bought it that if he gave it plenty to eat for the journey, it would lay an egg on the way. This was also meant as a joke but I was delighted when a letter came from his wife to say the hen had arrived safely with a big egg under it.

The Americans have added another name to my list. I have been called Milk Girl, Milk Woman, Milk Maid and they call me Milk Marm!

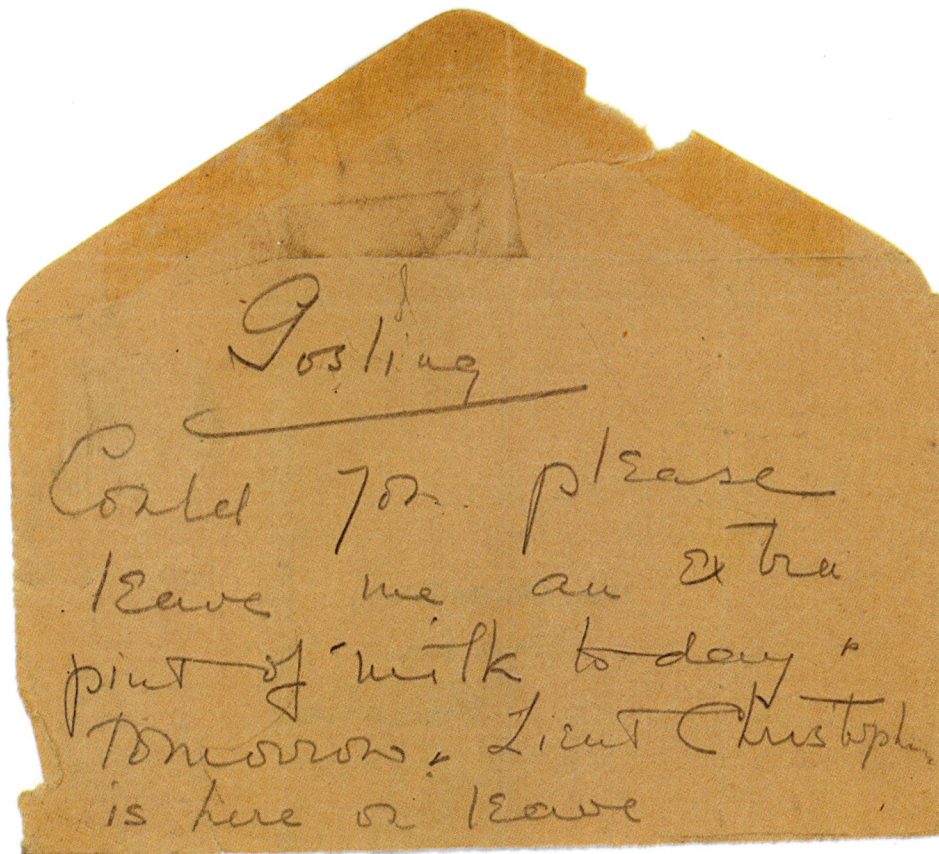

One of Anne's collection of doorstep notes.

May 15th

Farm

Like a flash, my month on the round passed by and I returned to the farm wondering which I really preferred. One of the things I do like about the farm is the uncertainty of what the day's programme will be. One never knows quite what may crop up and today was one of those days. One or two bombs dropped in the village during the night[52] and we were phoned to take milk down to the bombed-out people who were taken to a big house to be clothed and fed. There was the usual excitement accompanying a blitz, with rumours of who had been killed, who hurt, what sized bombs, etc. The Boss took us in his car and spent the morning chatting to important-looking wardens wearing tin hats and finally we drove round the country picking up crow bars from a blacksmith in the next village and odd jobs which filled in the morning.

Next day also, routine went to the winds. We had to go to the Park to chase out some straying heifers and divide up our own. We went down in the car. It was a lovely hot day and the Park looked magnificent, the trees at their very best, in full leaf, but not yet over-laden. Masses of white hay shone out among the green hedgerows and the sloping hillsides were "lit by the candelabra of horse-chestnut bloom." The pond, dark in the cool shade of great oaks, was a perfect scene with cows standing in the water knee-deep spreading ripples as they moved and others lying in the hot sunshine. It was a big job dividing them all up and sending them where they should go and we arrived home for lunch at a quarter to four. The cows go up to Queen's Meadow now in the evenings, where the grass is long and luscious again, and I always enjoy the walk there by winding paths through the forest. It also means the end of "haying-round" which was the last job to be done during the winter. Summer is really here.

But we need rain badly. The whole winter has been almost rainless and the ground is very dry. One day, when I was on the tractor discing, we had a day of showers. How refreshing they were. I have always been unable to describe my sense of real joy when rain came after a spell of very dry weather. And nobody has ever understood me when I told them that my skin and my whole being seemed to need the moisture. But now a writer to The Times has expressed it for me. He writes "The longing for rain becomes in time a physical sensation, above or below reason, and the first real shower brings a correspondingly rich physical relief." I felt that relief as I drove up and down and gladly watched the moisture soaking into the dry soil.

I am back on the tractor again and Elizabeth has a new twin sister whom I call Margaret Rose.[53] I like her better because I can put her into gear silently, but Elizabeth is more pliable. I have been working above Hollands Wood, where already part is sown with sugar beet and part with mangles. My stretch I prepared the ground for kale and while I was still rolling, old Arthur the gypsy came down with the horse drill. The scene tickled me. I could see the Boss on his tractor ploughing up the old kale. Here was I with my enormous rollers dragging behind me and Arthur looked like a clown in the circus when he arrived on the scene with the antiquated little wooden drill pulled by old "Dreadnought" and led solemnly by Arthur in his long, tattered, Dracula-like black coat and shrunken trilby hat, with young Eddy[54] walking behind the drill to see that it was seeding properly. However, it did its work, maybe slowly, but surely, and I have heard it said that the wise farmer uses horses in collaboration with tractors – as the Boss does. He uses horses for all muck-spreading and carting. He has three of them - Jumbo, Diana and Dreadnought – all powerful creatures who cost little in upkeep and who each do a good job of work each day.

Anne mentions three working horses on the farm. This earlier photo shows there were more.
The man on the far left is Walter Gossling. New Park Farm is in the background.

May Frosts

Old Joe shook his wise old head when the newspapers announced that the Ministry of Food had fixed the summer prices of fruit. "Shouldn't count their chickens before they're hatched", he muttered, and he was right. Hard May frosts have laid bare the wonderful trees of blossom which have billowed the countryside with rolling clouds of white and pink flowers. As I drove, standing up in my float, above the level of the hedges, I could see stretches of blossom spreading away on either side of me. It came to replace the early spring daffodils and crocus which came so soon and were so short lived. I think never had I seen such perfect blossom, especially the cherry, and variegated pink garden cherries which, as I say, were clouds of pink or white floating around the trees. And then in one night, the whole beauty was shattered. I woke to find a hard white frost spread across my moor and my sensations were a mixture of physical joy and mental pain. I could not help but feel the elation that comes with a sunny, frosty morning when the air is bright and keen, the more so after weeks of really hot weather and yet, I said to my heart "How dare you be glad, when you know what harm is being wrought". And when I looked at the lovely old apple trees standing there in our orchard, with blackened blossom, which yesterday was pink and crisp, like the artificial sprays one sees in a shop, I said why should Nature produce so abundantly and so generously, only to destroy? But I got no answer. Everyone was too saddened at the loss of their fruit which had promised a record crop. I did the round this morning and it was the only topic of the day. Everywhere I was shown frosted trees of apple, cherry and plum. Gooseberries, which were already formed the size of a small grape, had dropped in showers onto the ground under the bushes. Early potatoes hung limp and blackened and strawberries, large and even red, were ruined. What surprised me so much was that I heard hardly a grumble. That calamity (for it was nothing short of a calamity in these days of strict rationing when fruit is such a joy to add to a monotonous diet) seemed to crush rather than to anger. It was accepted with a resignation which was far more sad than wrath, as if Fate, which had already dealt so many hard blows, had just added another which must be accepted, like the rest unquestionably. I think we are well schooled in this after four years of war when our slogan has been never to help the enemy by grumbling. But it depressed me to find the whole countryside subdued and silent when I expected anger and vituperation.

One old cottager only a few days ago had shown me her potatoes and her gooseberries with great pride. "They'll be good this year", she said "one thing we never misses is new potatoes and gooseberry pie on a Whitsunday."[55] She'll miss them this year, but she never made a mention of it today. I expect it was too near her heart to do so.

Day after day, the frosts continued, harder and yet harder, till people who had laboriously hung newspapers over their lettuces and choice flowers, knew it was useless to struggle any more. The newspapers announced that the Ministry of Food were re-fixing the price of fruit.

Old Joe nodded his head. "I thought they were a bit quick", he said.

When I found that a lovely little calf, born yesterday, had died in the night, again said "Why, why, why?" and then I read a chapter about the cuckoo by Arthur C. Benson, who describes its unvarying instinct of stealing another bird's nest and destroying another bird's eggs as a "Satanically clever thing to do; such a strange fantastic whim of the creation to take thought in originating it."

He writes "One would expect a law, framed by omnipotence, to be invariable, not hampered by all kinds of difficulties that omnipotence, one might have thought, could have provided against. To make a law, as the Creator seems to have done and then to make a hundred other laws that seem to make the first law inoperative, to play this gigantic game century after century; and then to put into the hearts of our inquisitive race the desire to discover what it is all about; and to leave the desire unsatisfied. What a labyrinthine mystery! Depth beyond depth and circle beyond circle.

"Yet still I am no nearer the secret. God sends me, here the frozen peak, there the blue sea; here the tiger, there the cuckoo; here Virgil, there Jeremiah; here St. Francis of Assisi, there Napoleon. And all the while, as he pushes his fair or hurtful toys upon the stage, not a whisper, not a smile, not a glance escapes him; he thrusts them on, he lays them by; but the interpretation he leaves with us, and there is never a word out of the silence to show us whether we have guessed aright."

(from "The Thread of Gold" – Arthur C. Benson)[56]

May 18th

"Rogation" or "Farm Sunday"

This is Rogation, or Farm Sunday, when in olden times the Gospels were read in the corn fields, when our ancestors walked out into the fields in procession, parson and choir, in their white surplices, among the white hawthorn, and the people following; and the children carrying poles round which they had twisted all the flowers of May. And they would stand and read the Gospels in the corn. And ask a blessing on the corn and all the crops; on your corn and my corn and our neighbour's corn. And you, and I, and our neighbour would be there. We had worked hard for that corn. From as long ago as last harvest time, we had been working for it. Yet we felt that our work alone, our utmost, was not enough. We called on a power beyond our power. And the parson told his people, if any of them had a dispute with another to make it up and be friends as they walked together through the fields on Rogation Sunday.

So spoke Adrian Bell in today's Rogationtide address, but "Farm Sunday" has a very special and magical sound in my ears. It emphasises the difference between Sunday-on-the-farm and Sunday-on-the-milk-round. Every alternate month, I have Farm Sundays and how joyful they are! I go to bed the night before feeling relaxed at the thought of an easy day ahead with several hours of leisure in which to get done all my accumulation of odd jobs which have collected during the week. The cowmen get up earlier in order to be home in time for a good Sunday breakfast and when milking is finished and I have cleaned up in the dairy and fed the calves, I am gloriously free then till the second milking about 2 o'clock. I rush home to my chores and end the morning with a rather special lunch, which I have cooked the day before, with always a glass of cider in celebration, and leave a spotlessly clean house, with afternoon tea (a once a week treat) laid ready for my return.

There is a sense of gaiety also in our cowsheds on Sunday afternoon. Everyone has a "good dinner" and the atmosphere is benign. The farm children are home from school and they, with the gypsy children, crowd into the sheds to watch us milk. The young ones clamber about, climbing the rails and sliding in the fodder pen, a merry crew, while the older ones stand in a long silent line listening to our banter, dressed in their gayest clothes, a conglomeration of styles and colours achieved only by the gypsies. How they love the gaudiest hues! And I can never fathom where they keep their large selection, when it seems hardly possible that there is room for them, much less their clothes, in their diminutive tents. We have weekend campers too who come week after week, year after year and they delight to lend a hand and do odd jobs which all helps to get us away earlier, perhaps by four instead of five or six o'clock, so that the evening seems full of possibilities, the only evening in the week when one can have time to enjoy a sense of leisure. Every Farm Sunday is my Rogation Sunday, when I give thanks for everything!

May 23rd

Today, quite suddenly and out of the blue, came to me the secret of how to keep my tractor straight. I had not found it very difficult ploughing, for the Boss "strikes out" the first few furrows and then it is just a question of keeping one wheel of the tractor along the rut and the plough follows automatically. But surface work like rolling and discing is incredibly difficult for the great rollers or discs get a roll on them and swing out behind, causing the tractor to change direction continually. I have always prided myself on rather a straight eye and it depresses me enormously to find what uneven patterns I was printing on the soil. There was no hiding it. And after days of hard effort and concentration, I decided to resign myself to the inevitable and just accept that it was the best I could do. And now today, when I was making no effort, as so often happens, it suddenly came to me. I was driving with my right hand on the wheel and my arm resting firmly on my hip, which was turned slightly wheelwards, and I realised that in this way, I was keeping the tractor steady and straight. Previously I had driven with the wheel loose, so that at every bump, she changed direction and wobbled. By holding the wheel perfectly steady between my two hands and my arm forced against my hip, which had the whole force of my body behind it, the tractor took the bumps smoothly and when I looked behind, I saw perfectly straight and flawless tracks following in my wake. So often it is only when one has learnt how to do a thing properly that one realises how poor have been one's previous efforts and I blushed now when I remembered my other amateur efforts. I felt thrilled indeed with this new achievement and roared up and down over the rough ground with my discs following behind me and a song in my heart. Jack and the two boys were high up in the trees which skirted the edge of this field, a belt of forest cut off in a straight line. They were lopping off the great overgrowing branches which cast a shadow and I was glad they had such a good bird's eye view of my work, which seemed really almost flawless. And then the Boss came, to follow me with the rollers. I saw him look but he said nothing. I needed no words of praise. I knew it was good. Closer and closer he came to me till his great rollers covered the whole ground I had disced and then he waited, sitting on his tractor watching me with a smile of indulgence, as I laboriously completed the triangle at the last corner and I am sure that my grin of triumph when I finished and drove homewards conveyed my delight.

John Stewart Collis[57] in a lovely article in "Time and Tide" called "The Plough" asks why it should matter so much whether you can plough a "straight furrow." "Why should it matter so much, seeing all the lines will presently be knocked to pieces under the harrow?" He thinks the real reason is aesthetic. "It is the tribute that Agriculture pays to Art. It is felt that there is virtue in a straight line, not to be found in one that wobbles even slightly. This calls for concentration and skill. Where there is skill, there is art; where there is art, there is passion for the absolute. The straight furrow is the labourer's acknowledgement of the validity in art for art's sake."

But I don't agree with him! It is obvious that unless one works straight, one cannot disc or roll or plough the ground evenly. You see when you rule a page with lines which are not straight how soon the spaces at the edge become uneven and how at the end, a large area is left waste. Even more so in a great field 30 or 40 acres in size. It is only by keeping straight that one can be sure of working it all over properly. The agriculturist seeks perfection not from any aesthetic sense but to achieve the results which only thoroughness can give.

Personalities

I think what has set me wondering most of all during this past year is the personality of the animals and how individual each one is. It seems less amazing in people. We take that for granted. Even so, it was brought to me most forcibly at Christmas when I retired to Galloway after 12 years and rediscovered my friends essentially unchanged. Some mature who had been young, some now elderly, but all had retained their own especial individuality, and all aroused the same response in me, which made me realise that the essential "me" in myself was unchanged also. An astounding fact really, in such a changing life, when even our very skins had almost changed twice. It seemed to prove to me the immortality of the soul more than anything else.

Most people would describe a herd of cows as a collection of placid, perhaps loveable, but most certainly rather dull and very similar creatures. As a matter of fact, scarcely two cows in our herd of 45 are the least alike and a collection of 45 people could hardly be more dissimilar. You have only to drive them from Queen's Mead to the farm for several mornings to realise what a very definite personality each one has. There is always the same cow who leads, who waits for the gate to be opened and then stalks ahead with determined air, looking neither to right nor left, her mind fixed on the stall she left behind the night before. Would they were all like her! There is the cow at the other end of the field, "Old General," who refuses to approach the gate till she is rounded up. All the way she lags behind, always at the very end of the long procession. You may hurry her for a few yards, but the moment you leave her side, her feet drag, and once more she falls behind. There is the disagreeable, who stands unfailingly on the little wooden bridge, barring the way of those who follow and butting them viciously with her horns. There are the greedy ones, several of them, who cannot bear to pass the tender tufts of grass which grow beneath the bracken, or fresh young beech leaves which bend beside the stream. They stand and guzzle till they are whacked onwards, reluctantly dragging a last mouthful by the roots with eyes always searching for more ahead. There are young Patchy and old Peggy who, day after day, wander through the bracken across inaccessible parts of the river to the moor beyond. Day after day, they have to be chased and brought back, but they never mend their ways. Once the cowsheds are in sight, there are the cows who enter gladly, who walk up to their stalls as soldiers fill their ranks. There are those who loiter around the corners and wander among the stables, those who invariably take up their stand in the wrong stall in the hopes of finding a better feed in their neighbour's than their own. And always you can hear little Dora and Dilly, two Guernseys, running the whole length of the cowshed, because although they are late, they are determined not to be last!

And then their varied personalities become very evident when you start to milk. You find the "hard" cows who refuse to let their milk down unless intimidated or persuaded; the easy gracious milkers who are no trouble to anyone and whom I fear have the roughest handling because they are invariably handed to beginners! The fidgety and nervous ones who will not stand still and who flick their tails across your face, either from sheer irritability or from fear. And lastly the kickers who have to be tied and who scarcely ever mend their ways – "once a kicker, always a kicker." An interesting collection when you know them and yet "they are so unintelligent in some regions, so subtly wise in others", an observation on cows made by A. C. Benson and so profoundly true in connection with our "Round" ponies. It is almost uncanny how they can know each stopping place by instinct, yet how utterly at sea they can be if their route is changed. And they, all of them, have their own very distinct personality. Danny is the greedy one who will do anything, go anywhere, for a morsel of food and who will kick viciously if it is denied her. She is rough and shaggy and full-out. She will trot from house to house merrily as if she enjoyed her work as much as her food. Brownie is the staid, reliable old lady who never loses sight of her dignity, who moves always at her own pace, who can never be whipped up or hurried, who will stand for an hour on end till she hears the gate click, then she turns her face and when she is sure you are ready to go on, she will move. But strange contradiction! When she is loose in a field, she can never be caught. Two dozen yards of rope must be tied to her halter and almost flawlessly can she judge that distance of two dozen yards between you and herself and freedom. Peter, my favourite, is the least reliable and the most nervous and I regret to admit the least intelligent. When he puts his mind to it, he can be perfect, but he can also be exasperatingly stupid and most erratic. Any quick or excited movement terrifies him and once frightened, he is the very devil to calm down. Anything unusual at the side of the road, like a new puddle of water or a fallen branch, causes him to shy and upsets him for a considerable time. He has little fortitude in discomfort and refuses to stand if flies worry him or if spots of rain drop onto him from a tree. He dislikes dark shadowy places and hates to stand in such. It is the greatest difficulty to get him to trot up to the end of a closed road. Slower and slower he gets and finally has to be led the last few yards. Yet there is something appealing about him which has captured my affection. There is a pathetic quality in all the animals which is expressed by A. C. Benson when he writes "They are so unconscious of the sad reasons for which we desire their company – so unsuspicious! So serene! Instead of learning by sorrowful experience of generations what our dark purposes are, they become more and more fraternal, more and more dependent."

June 6th

D-Day

My month on the milk round started again just as our preparations for the Invasion of the Continent were ended. Last time I was on the road, all was a swirl of traffic, a grim mass of troops and vehicles bound for secret destinations, relentlessly moving forward to bring us victory, but at what cost one dared not think. Miles of convoys stood parked at the roadsides, covered with camouflage netting and branches of trees. Every "Cover" was teeming with hidden troops, who walked out into the village in the evenings and filled the streets with ribaldry. The feeling of tension grew more and more unbearable as day after day passed with not a sign of our Second Front being opened up.[58] One longed for something to happen to get this dread waiting over, like some ghastly operation which must be performed and yet one was instinctively thankful each day, when it did not come. And then suddenly, there was a great silence and the day I started my round again, I found the roads hushed and empty. There were no troops, no traffic, no hold-ups to let convoys pass. The sun shone and the village was still with a great stillness. Never have I felt a greater tension. The shops were empty. The housewives, instead of jabbering over counters or in the coffee shop, stayed at home waiting for news and meanwhile I drove my float through empty streets and filled my jugs at closed doors.

Bill Cuthbertson Calbert, a Canadian soldier. He was the close friend of Robert (Bob) Comber, another Canadian soldier who came to the New Forest. They were both serving with the Queen's Own Rifles of Canada. Freda Sque was to marry Bob and move with him to Canada: she has lived there ever since. Her daughter, Sue, sent this photograph of Bill. It shows him in the New Forest shortly before D-Day. Bob Comber described the horror when Bill was disembarking on the French coast and was killed instantly: "As Bill and his crew left the barge in their carrier on June 6th heading for the beach at Beny-Sue-Mer they fouled a sea mine and became a blinding ball of flames and twisted steel sizzling in the sea. It was a hard thing for me to watch from the shore. Only then did I realise what was taking place around me. The wreckage was vast and startling, the terrible waste and destruction of war, and loss of human life. Anything and everything became expendable." Bill was twenty-two.

On June 6th, news came through on the 7 o'clock broadcast that our troops had invaded Normandy and almost simultaneously, the weather changed. Weeks of glorious golden sunshine and blue skies gave way to grey clouds and rain and then a demon wind sprang up – a wind which never stopped blowing for days on end, with swirling dark clouds, a wind which we all knew was tossing our ships as they made their way across the Channel and clouds which were making it impossible for our aircraft to give them the air support which was so necessary. We held our breaths and waited and prayed. At every house, people would come to the door and hold their jugs for me to fill, looking dimly at the sky and murmuring "Our poor boys! Is there any sign of change?"

However, despite the weather[59], we made our landing and held our ground and advanced. Mothers who had only a few days before received a parcel of their son's "personal belongings" were reassured by the arrival of postcards and letters written from the very beaches of Normandy. The whole atmosphere became normal again as our spirits rose. We were doing marvellously in Italy and the Russians were sweeping in from the east. "Hitler was cornered at last" and with true British optimism we all agreed that it was only a matter of time. Speculation was rife as to how long it would take to get to Berlin with the fervent hope that the Russians would reach there first.

Traffic now commenced to swirl the other way. Long lines of Red Cross ambulances driving back the wounded and covered trucks of prisoners sweeping inland. Guns could be heard thundering across the Channel and the whirring of big bombers droning out of sight above the grey clouds.

My route had to be altered to conform with the new one way traffic. We had to divide up the two rounds, which meant learning new houses and meeting new customers, which was a welcome change, except that my round was made longer (too long) and I had to leave second, which meant I had to milk and fill all the bottles before I left. It took some time to resign myself to this, as previously I had delighted in setting off early with plenty of time to spare. Now I was dependent on a number of milkers as to what time I should start and the first flush of my energy was used up before I started. And worst of all was I had to take what milk was left and when it was short, I had to suffer. It was short. Several of the cows were drying off and I was forced to cut down my customers, which is always unpleasant. However I soon realised it was all in a day's work and I must make the best of a bad job and I found some quaint new people to deal with, who cheered me up. One, Mrs Martin, who lived in a mental home for thirty years and who was so glad to get out again that she has tried to make everybody else "happy" ever since. She would have the pot ready to share a cup of tea with me the minute I called every day, with always a bunch of roses, or a lily stalk lying beside her jug for me to take away. Old Mrs Penfold also is slightly queer, much to the inconvenience of her neighbours, because she steals the notes they leave on their doorsteps for the tradesmen and they are their wits end to know how to do their ordering. Every day when I call, she says she must pay me and goes away to find the money, returning in a few minutes to say that her husband has stolen it from her drawer. Actually he, who is the coalman, and a right grimy one too, pays me regularly every Saturday and tapping his forehead significantly as he looks in the direction of his wife he whispers "Don't take no notice of her. She be a bit funny here." She calls me Miss Curly Head and appears supremely happy in her senselessness. Mr Clare, the picture framer, is quite blind. He comes every day to the door with a smile on his face bringing me the jug, which he receives again between open, sensitive hands and stands chatting about the day's events in such a normal way.

My sudden appearance at these new houses was a cause of great interest and I was conscious of eyes behind curtains. Several thought I must be Mrs Gossling. One thought I looked "Russian" and one said that if I were Scotch, she'd never seen a Scotchwoman like me before! At one house I went to, two little girls were playing in the garden and when I opened the gate, the younger one ran screaming to her mother. "I don't like the new Milk Girl!" she yelled, "she's got a funny face." "Do you think I've got a funny face?" I asked her sister, who nodded her head silently, "then why do you think it's funny?" I persisted. "I don't know" she answered "but it is!"

It is perplexing, when one has considered oneself a perfectly normal individual to be regarded as somebody rather strange. But I have retained a large proportion of my original customers and they seem very familiar and friendly when I visit them.

A doorstep note to the milk lady that speaks for itself with beautiful handwriting.

June 18

The Doodle Bug

Just when we were so confident that we had Hitler "nicely in the bag", he launched his secret weapon, V1, a flying bomb which propelled itself mainly in the direction of London, but occasionally over our heads. "Hitting below the belt, that's what I calls it" observed an old gamekeeper "just when we thought we'd got him beat."

Information was very scarce as to the real state of affairs in London. The wireless and the papers revealed nothing and friends letters were more than reticent. However, gradually, news began to leak through and we began to realise that although it could never win the war, the p-plane[60] could be distinctly disagreeable. There was a factor of uncanniness about it which horrified the imagination and, although one called it "The Doodle Bug" and laughed it was really nothing to be amused at.

Our first one fell in the early hours of one morning. I was asleep. I didn't even hear it coming, but I heard it explode and very near to me it was, but luckily in an open space. I opened my eyes and murmured "the Doodle Bug" and turned over and went to sleep again because I was very tired.

Excitement was rife next morning. I, being the first visitor of the day at every house, had to stand and hear everyone's description of what each had heard and seen. It had flown straight over every house, be it situated north, south, east or west. It had shut off its engine above every rooftop and some people had seen yellow flashes and others a red glow. My milk delivery got later and later till at last I was sick of the very name of Doodle Bug.

More came over at intervals and people began to sleep in their shelters, or bring their beds down to the basement. Children were sent from London to live here with relations, but no-one lost confidence for a moment that it was only a stunt weapon and could never win the war. We were sure also that there couldn't be many more, but there was one more anyway which, but for the fraction of a split second, might have meant the end of my milk round. This one did come right over the roof of the farmhouse, blowing open every door and cracking windows as it went. It shut off its engine directly above the roof and glided, turning slightly leftwards to explode at the far side of the dairy field. The poor old cows ran like blazes and the big cart horses and the ponies careered madly round the field, kicking their heels in the air. It is generally assumed that if cows are made to hurry, they yield less milk, but our milk was "up" after this little incident!

The gypsies' camp is in the adjoining field and they were terrified. The mother gypsy said she picked up her baby and flung herself and it into the ditch and her daughters were so angry with her because she didn't take all their babies because they were too frightened to move!

Old Joe sat up in bed as it came over, bursting open his front door and he heard the voice of his 4 year old nipper through the darkness saying "That's pigeon shooting Dad, that is!"

Anne, on her way to work, must have seen the Forest trees standing in water like this after extended periods of rain.
Photograph by Christopher Andreae

June 20

Start Haymaking

This regrettable weather, which has been holding up our Invasion, has also held up haymaking. We had a drought for so long, indeed there has been no rain to speak of all winter and all spring has been so dry, that there is scarcely any hay to cut and when the rains came, it was so necessary for our root crops that it was difficult to know whether to be pleased about it for the crops or sorry about it for the hay. Anyway, it doesn't matter much if we are pleased or sorry because we just have to take it as it comes and, contrary to the usual idea that "farmers always grumble about the weather," I never hear the Boss make a complaint, nor the cowmen either. They just look up at the sky and observe that it will rain or it will be fine and there it ends at that. I find that I am the only one who grouses, because it seems to me so vital to have the right weather at the right moment, but I think the farmers realise that somehow, however bad it looks at the time, it all seems to come right in the end. And this is what happened with our hay. We cut the clover field and a poor thin crop it was too and picked it up all in a matter of 2 or 3 days, and cut the hay field and that very night the weather changed again and for 3 weeks we had rain day after day, with the result that after the fine spell, the rain brought in the rest of the hay and the wheat began to flourish visibly, especially our winter wheat, which began to look exceptionally fine and very lovely when the sun shone on it, giving it a soft blue sheen. This mingling of blue and green against a blue sky is an equally beautiful sight as a broad field of ripe golden corn.

Indeed, it is perhaps more subtle and more fleeting than the cruder contrasts of gold and blue. I think it is overlooked because people are so apt to be too used to green. They accept it without looking at the multitudinous shades and hues of green, which range green, which range from almost yellow to deepest olive, passing through a scale of grey-greens, blue-greens and softest greeny-white where leaves are turned backwards, shining in a bright light. White is a neglected colour also, but to me, there are a thousand different whites and each is so valuable wherever it is placed. White cherry blossom falling in sprays around a black tall trunk. Masses of white May in June hedges blending into the soft young greens of the early summer, white ox-eye daisies gleaming among yellow buttercups and long meadow grass, the white markings of cows, which are either black or red, picking them out amongst the green soft pastures and white clouds in a blue sky – and white clothes hanging from a line. White gives a great vitality to any scene and a mixed bowl of flowers should always contain 2 or 3 white blooms. I usually add these at the very end and it is extraordinary what a unity they achieve.

In spite of the rain though, our kale was a complete failure. Acres of it were no good. The gypsies transplanted the few roots which survived the drought and the nest I disced over and rolled, preparatory to sowing turnips. It is too late to sow more kale.

I had a week's "rest" on the farm and enjoyed it so much, on the tractor most of every day, distributing fertiliser on the pastures and also where we have cut our hay. The Boss has decided that instead of trying for a second crop of hay, he will induce a good winter crop and give it to the cows in pasture rather than in hay. The papers already predict a short supply of milk for next year. We have no kale, very little hay. We have used these last weeks a considerable amount of our winter cake ration. So we must rely on turnips and good winter pasture.

Here are the same June gardens, a riot of sweet Williams, phloxes, lavender, roses trailing over every trellis and orange marigolds. Each drive I walk up is deep-scented with honeysuckle and buddleia, a scent so strong in my memory from last year when I came to it so suddenly from city life. It is all the same – even the vegetable gardens planted with the same rows of lettuces, peas and beans and carrots. Bushes still hanging with black and red currants and luscious raspberries and scarlet runners climbing up tall stakes. And once again, old Mr Gulliver provides my "daily ration" of 3 pods placed on his kitchen table beside his jug. He put them there for me every day last June and now every day I find them again and every day I think "I have been filling this jug for a whole year now." It has been a good year, a year of great gain because in it I have learnt to know the seasons. I have sensed the satisfaction of physical exhaustion and the joy of relaxation after a hard day's work. I have learnt the control imposed by relentless routine and I believe I have almost learnt the futility of looking ahead and worrying about events which may never happen. I am content to take each day as it comes, as the farmer does, and deal with it to the best of my ability and tackle each problem when it arises.

I know that I have acquired a philosophy and a confidence in life which I hope I shall be able to retain when I have left the land. I have learnt it from the men who live on the land and I have learnt it from the land itself. As Walter Rose writes "How could man move amid that process, and have that vast operation taking place daily before his eyes, without having his whole life influenced by it? The farmer and his men understood that unison of the soil with the elements and recognised that they themselves were the agents through whom nature alone could fulfil that function. They knew that the . . . plough, with their hands in control, was an essential part of an unchanging purpose that involved their thoughts and efforts. This understanding, which they expressed in their own way, was the source of the farmer's stable outlook on life, and of the labourers' patience and contentment."[61]

I should like to conclude my year on the farm by quoting the psalm of Harvest Thanksgiving.

"He bringeth forth grass for the cattle and green herbs for the service of men, that he may bring food out of the earth and wine that maketh glad the heart of man and oil to make him a cheerful countenance and bread to strengthen man's heart."[62]

I have seen these things happening for a whole year and I know that they must continue while the earth exists.

Farm Flippancy

We have days of high hilarity as well as days of deep gloom in our cowsheds. These moods are not confined to youth who is so easily cast down and so quickly elated to radiant heights! Old Joe too is as changeable as the English climate and after days of highest elation we will suddenly see him sitting like a "green and yellow melancholy"[63] beneath a cow and then all our spirits droop and we milk in a subdued silence waiting for the storm to burst, for on these occasions he gets rid of his own spleen by attacking us. Nothing we can do on these occasions is right and most unjustly he condemns us for our every action and if we dare to argue then the fat is in the fire indeed. Poor Joe, over-eating is his weakness! He gourmandises for weeks till nature's safety valve does its work and he is laid up for a day or so with his usual malady. "Joe's not here?" we say when we see his empty place, "sick again, I suppose, the pig!" we declare and his patient wife[64] seizes her opportunity for sympathy and regales us with blood freezing descriptions of the enormous dishes he demands for his dinners. Several pounds of potatoes and 2 or 3 cabbages must accompany his meat every day. Once she presented me with a great paper hat-bag full of mushrooms which would have provided the normal family with a meal for several days and when I hesitated to accept them because I was sure Joe would like them, she laughed heartily and said "Oh Joe wouldn't look at these – he'd want three times as much for one meal!" He had three times as many the other day and paid his usual price, which we shared in having to do his work! However, once relieved of his internal burden, he is as merry as a cricket and there is no holding him and on those days there is great fun and laughter and real wit bubbling in our cowsheds.

It was on one of these occasions that I formed the "O.O.A." – Our Own Army![65] Eileen and I were the only two girls not members of the W.L.A. – Woman's Land Army – and I must admit we felt a trifle out of it when the local representative came periodically to present the others with stripes and badges and when parcels of clothes and treasured Wellington boots and magazines came for them and nothing for us. On this day,

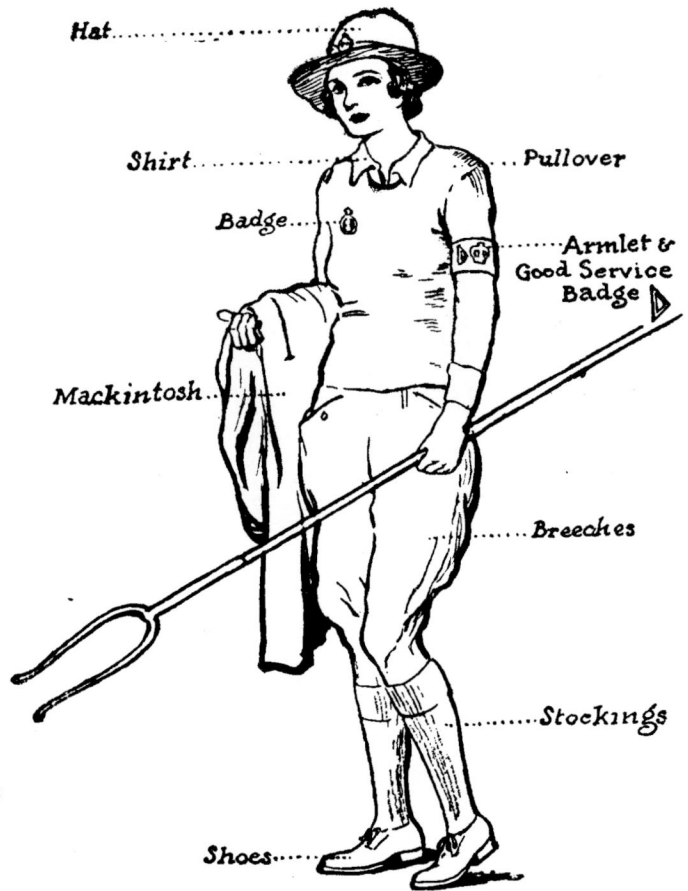

©The estate of W.E. Shewell-Cooper 2011 and the Amberley Archive. 'The Uniform for the Land Girl' from *A Manual for Volunteers in the Women's Land Army* by W.E. Sherwell-Cooper was published in 1941. This is one of two line drawings in it which showed the uniforms they were to wear. This Manual was recently re-published, by Amberley Publishing, as an "amazing period piece."

Dorothy stalked in proudly with a third, new stripe on her arm and it suddenly occurred to me that Eileen and I should form our own opposition Army. We discussed it while we were milking and Joe thought it was a grand idea. We became more and more flippant, selecting ridiculous titles, but finally decided to call ourselves the "O.O.A." – Our Own Army. That evening, I rooted in my odd scrap drawer and discovered a large piece of American cloth, shining white on one side and crimson felt on the other. It was the very thing! I cut it in strips for armlets – the crimson uppermost – and stuck absurd white jagged shapes for year and half yearly stripes, with O.O.A. painted in large black letters above. Next morning, we entered the cowsheds together with these things buttoned onto our arms. They looked amazingly decorative and official on our overall coats and took the place by storm. Eileen

This is the most usual armband worn by members of the Women's Land Army, with red details on a green background. This is featured in Anne Kramer's book *Land Girls and Their Impact*. These armbands meant a lot to the land girls. Each half-diamond chevron represented six months service.

wore a crimson spotted scarf round her head and I knotted a crimson kerchief round my neck which just completed the musical comedy effect. What a reception we got! Old Joe and Jack caught onto the idea like wildfire and in a few minutes, the O.O.A. was well away. The Boss also was vastly amused and entered into this ribaldry with unexpected enthusiasm. Eileen wore hers on the milk round where it caused quite a furore and I wore mine on the farm. Everyone was terribly impressed, especially the gypsies, when I told them in all seriousness that we belonged to a "different Land Army." However, soon the situation became serious because Joe and Jack, with their distorted sense of humour, began to boost the O.O.A. to the disadvantage of the W.L.A. and the W.L.A. didn't appreciate the humour of it all. Any difficult job that had to be tackled was given to us to do and any mistakes that were made were blamed on the others "because the O.O.A. would never do a thing like that"! Joe, who has really a clever wit, made cruel jibes at the others in favour of us and before long, the W.L.A. had all its glory torn in tatters and the O.O.A. reigned supreme! Eileen and I shook in our shoes as we watched Dorothy, Freda and co getting more and more angry. We made faces at Joe and clenched our fists silently at him when he saw his humour bursting forth, but this of course only added to his enthusiasm and the tension grew so great that reluctantly we agreed we must lose our armlets and let "Our Own Army" die a natural death. Peace reigned for a few days till Sarah,[66] one of the gypsy girls, came to me and asked if she might join our army. It happened that this was the very day when Eileen had earned a new stripe for an extra year's work, so I cut out another zigzag white shape and Joe made a presentation of it in the cowshed. He presented it to her on an upturned bucket, with due ceremony, and made a lovely (and to Sarah!) a most impressive speech and then spat on the back of the stripe and planked it onto her armlet in the name of Hour Hown Harmy! And that night, I made another armlet for Sarah which I put in a large "On His Majesty's Service" envelope, with a covering letter enrolling Sarah as a new recruit. She had already worked on the farm for two years, so I gave her two broad stripes. Her delight, when it arrived by post, knew no bounds. She can just read and was greatly impressed by the typewritten, official-looking letter and for the first time in her life she began to work with real enthusiasm. There was no holding her. She came early and worked late and her whole face shone with pride and joy. But to our horror, instead of wearing her armlet for work, it was so precious that she kept it folded in its envelope during working hours and paraded the village with it every evening! I was terrified someone would disillusion her and tell her it all a cruel hoax, so once again Eileen and I decided to lose our armlets and forget it – but not so Sarah. And Joe and Jack were doubled up with mirth every time they saw her. It was distinctly uncomfortable for us, because she now regarded me as a sort of fairy godmother who had initiated her into this grand concern and every day she would smile at me with eyes full of dog-like gratitude and emotion and bring me presents of flowers and watercress, which she had gathered. I felt something must be done, but I couldn't think what. Things boiled to a head one afternoon when we were driving with the Boss to the village. It was Sarah's half day and there we passed her on the main road, dressed in her best clothes with her crimson armlet glaring on her arm in the middle of the group of admiring friends and soldiers. I felt quite sick with horror at my deceit and the Boss himself grew pink and almost angrily said to me "Anne, you'll have to tell her – she'll be getting herself into trouble".

For two whole days, I cogitated as to how I could divorce her from that armlet without utter disillusionment. I always believe that if only one thinks long enough, one can always find the answer and in the quiet watches of the night, I found mine!

I wrote her another letter [see overleaf], typewritten of course, and signed by the Head of the O.O.A. to say that in view of the opening up of our Second Front and widespread movement of troops to the continent, it was found necessary to recall all armlets lest they should cause confusion in military operations. I used the longest and most impressive words I could think of and added my gratitude for her faithful work in the war effort and my conviction that she would "continue her good work with unabated zeal." I posted the letter and felt I had been really inspired! When Sarah read it, she ran all the way up to the fields to her tent and returned "to hand it in to me" (as requested) still folded in its original tissue paper, with tears in her eyes, and she has hardly done a stroke of work since!

Now, when she hangs about loafing, as of old, and fails to turn up at the weekends and the Boss grumbles, I say to him "Well it's all your fault, you made me disband the O.O.A." – and he can't help grinning. It just shows what medals and ribbons can achieve.

The real land army girls on the farm started to be annoyed by Anne's bit of fun at their expense, and her own imaginary counter-organisation, O.O.A. (Our Own Army) was relegated to the history books.

Horns

Sally, one of our cows, cast a horn which I found at the foot of a straw stack when I was driving them out to graze. I kept it and wondered what I could do with it to keep it as a memento and I finally decided to set it on a wooden plaque to form a hook for hats and coats in my hall. The ever-willing Joe produced a panel from his old wireless set. It was just the thing and when the horn was duly washed and varnished and inset, it looked really lovely. And now I decided I must make a collection and have at least three in a row, with each cow's name written in small brass nails underneath each horn.

HOLEBROOK HOUSE.

SEE MY ROOM AT THE TOP!
& THE ANTIQUE SHOP BELOW.
        THE GAP AT THE SIDE IS WHERE
        THE GYPSIES GATHER WITH THEIR
        PONIES & CARTS. THEY SELL
        WATER LILIES & AFTERWARDS
        BUY WAR SAVINGS CERTIFICATES
                AT THE POST OFFICE!

Anne lived in the centre of Brockenhurst on Brookley Road, in the top floor room of a quaint house that remains there today –
these days with a hairdresser at street level. This is her watercolour of the house. It is still called Holbrook House, though
spelled differently from how it was in Anne's day.

To my delight, not many weeks later, Tiny came in for milking minus her horn and the whole farm was incited to search for it. I offered each of the gypsy boys a packet of cigarettes if they could find it for me and not long passed before Henry produced a horn, which he said was Tiny's, but which I am doubtful about as it looks old and dry and in no way corresponds to her existing horn in any shape or size or colour! However, I accepted it in the spirit in which it was given and was pleased to have two to start my row. Tuesday was market day and the Boss returned from Salisbury with a new cow. There is always a good deal of excitement when a new cow arrives and we all go to inspect it to see what kind of milker she is likely to be and this day, when we were trooping off, Dorothy (who had been at the buy) said to me "Pop bought her for you Anne, because of her horns. He says you can hang your whole wardrobe on them!" and indeed I almost could! They are the most magnificent, wide spreading horns, and so long! And Joe and I have discussions every so often as to how we can get one of them off for my collection. I take a special interest in her and though she has proved disappointing from a milk point of view, I say "Well she was worth £30 for her horns". She is registered in the official chart as "Horny" and I do hope I can get hold of one of those horns one day – as a memento.

I have since achieved two more from a poor old cow who collapsed on her way home from Queen's Mead with red water fever, a deadly germ which suddenly attacks the bloodstream and weakens the whole system in a few hours. She was unable to walk home and I was sent up in the evening to take her hay and water and "milk her out". I found her lying on her side in the bracken, her face thickly covered with flies while the sun poured down scorching her body. Her breath was coming quickly and her mouth was parched. I gave her a drink and milked her out into the grass as she lay there and then covered her up with branches of beech leaves and hung my yellow jacket from her horns to protect her from those "cruel flies feasting at her bloodshot eyes waiting for her heart to die." A few hours later she was dead, poor thing, and next day carted to the kennels in a great wagon to be cut up into flesh for the foxhounds. Arthur, who drove her there, sought me on his return, with her horns in his pocket, which I exchanged for two packets of cigarettes. I shall always feel sad when I think of Dora's unhappy end. She was a placid uninteresting creature, but I have a special affection for her because I was the last one to milk her and shared her distress.

June 23

Midsummer Madness

Although Midsummer's day was grey and bleak and not a bit the magical day it should be, nevertheless Puck must have been up to his pranks, for the most amazing madness took charge of our farm. Olive was washing bottles in the dairy and fell in love at sight with a swarthy young man who came to her for a pint of milk. He was camping with an Anglican priest and some boy scouts and a curate in the dairy field and in three days they were engaged and all set to be married in another month! As Harold is the priest's adopted son, Olive was quickly gathered into his fold to be married by him. One weekend she was baptised, the next confirmed and two weeks later was to be married. We reeled under the shock. Such dozens of young men swarmed around Olive that we hardly believed this could be serious and having declared herself strictly an atheist and a communist, it was difficult to picture her in this wealthy, ultra-religious atmosphere. However she just took no heed of anyone and kept telling me that Harold was "lovely" in her strong Lancashire voice. It was the speed of the thing and jealousy for her own daughter which made the farmer's wife incensed with fury and Olive was duly removed at a day's notice to a farm several miles away. My invitation to the wedding arrived next week printed in silver letters and looked very grand, but 3 days before the wedding, it was cancelled. Olive's brother, who is her guardian, had reconsidered his opinion and decided she was too young and must wait a year. The farmer's wife breathed a sigh of relief. Her dear Dorothy had not been outrun after all, but midsummer was not finished and Dorothy entered the cowshed one Sunday afternoon and fell in love with an American soldier who had come up to help us to milk. Things moved as rapidly as with Olive and all the nasty things which were said about Olive could not be applied to Dorothy! The farmer's wife was distraught, lest her darling should be whisked away to America. She wandered about in tears imploring providence to "end the war soon and send all these Americans back to their own country." She said she hoped he would get killed and never come back and finally descended to declaiming everything American. Every American programme on the wireless was switched off with anger and everything American was criticised. The poor young man was kept outside the house. I had to open up my own doors and offer hospitality out of sheer national shame. The Boss, kept awake at nights by his wrath-stricken wife, appealed to me to try and "make her see sense." She only wept and begged me to cajole with Dorothy and Dorothy and Larry continued to walk blissfully in Elysian fields and took no heed of anyone, till he disappeared as suddenly as he came into the battle fields of Normandy, leaving Dorothy writing letters to him every day and receiving no answers.

Meanwhile, Freda, who now visited my soldiers' mess on her new milk round, delivered milk to a fair young soldier of 18 years, fell madly in love with him and jilted Sonny, all in the space of a few days. Had her hair cut and "permed" and developed from a simple country maid into quite a young lady of fashion and not oblivious to her own charm at all. I remembered what an old lady once said; "There is nothing we can do in a love affair except to sit back and wait to pick up the bits". So I am just sitting back and wondering where it will all end.

Barbara[67]

Olive was duly replaced by Barbara and handed over to me to teach her my milk round. No two people could have been more different – and equally exasperating! Olive ruthless, impatient and dynamic and Barbara more placid than anyone I have ever met, sentimental and dreamy. Nothing on earth could make her move quickly or think quickly and I thought I should go dotty trying to make her realise that everything must be done on the run in order to get it done at all. She was all up in the clouds, enjoying every minute of it, but oh so slow! She is passionately fond of animals and spent her time conjecturing what Brownie might think of this or that and what she liked or disliked. Whenever I tried to jog her up into a decent trot, Barbara would turn on me in fury and seize the whip out of my hand with a crimson face, exclaiming that "poor Brownie was so old she couldn't hurry." I know Brownie[68] is old, but I also know that she is as cunning as a fox and quite cute enough to go slowly on purpose. I gave up the unequal struggle and let Brownie meander along at a snail's pace, while Barbara murmured "I could do this forever and a day, it's so peaceful." It was far from peaceful to me, who realised all the work waiting at the farm to be done when I got back and everyone there champing with wrath at our delay.

We passed cows grazing in the forest and Barbara asked "Aren't those cows big enough to give milk?" and I explained that it was really nothing to do with their size. Again, she asked how old Brownie was and when I answered "about twenty", she said "Then why do you call her a pony, surely she's old enough to be a horse!"

She followed me from house to house with a seraphic smile always on her face as I explained who lived there and what she must leave. When I got back home, I said to the Boss "I really don't know if she took in anything or nothing but I shall know better tomorrow." She was already the joke of the farm, but I discovered next day she was not such a fool as she looked. She had taken it all in, in her slow dreamy way and had really absorbed it.

After 4 days tuition, I gladly handed the reins into her eager hands. She longed to have Brownie to herself, who would treat her kindly and not bully her. And that day, she arrived home just before 6 p.m. instead of before 2! But it didn't worry her. She was perfectly happy and continued day after day at the same rate. Customers champed and phoned the farm to say they must have their milk earlier. Everyone at the farm grumbled and groused because, of course, she did no work when she got home. The Boss and his wife said she must leave, that she was quite impossible, and I was the only one who stuck up for her. I said "She is slow, but she does it well. She's honest and conscientious and you might do a thousand times worse." So here she is, still meandering along at her own speed, but never put out, and always happy and cheerful. Everything that could go wrong has gone wrong. Her harness has broken several times, her wheel came off, her shaft broken, the milk turned sour day after day and an acute shortage owing to evacuees, but nothing seems to disturb her equanimity and I can't help admiring her and feeling that perhaps after all she has "chosen the better part."[69]

She is engaged to a soldier who, when he departed to Normandy, wrote her a last letter telling her all he wanted to say in case he were killed. Soon after D-Day he dropped the letter and someone picked it up and posted it. Poor Barbara of course thought he must be killed and mourned for 5 days, when she received another letter from Bill and realised what had happened.

On her day off, when I arrive at houses about 3 hours earlier, the customers can hardly believe their eyes. One explained "Christ Almighty! There's the milk girl!"

September 16

Harvesting Again

Today we have gathered in the last remnants of our harvest. We cut our first wheat on August 9th and since then I have not had a minute to record anything. But it has been, as the Boss woefully remarked, "One long drawn-out agony." This year, unlike last year, which was straight sailing from beginning to end, simply everything that could go wrong went wrong.

First we were held up by our late hay and when we should have started harvesting, we were still haymaking. The winter wheat was really over-ripe when we cut it and the minute we cut it, rain came and days and days we spent stooking up drenching sheaves. It was just beginning to dry off fit for carrying when the sudden hot spell boiled up into a violent thunderstorm, which bashed the aisles to the ground and tossed out the ears. When we lifted the sheaves a day or so later, we found they had grown long whiskers into the stubble. It was heartbreaking to see our winter wheat ruined because it was an exceptionally rich crop. The spring sowing was poor and thin in any case because of the dry seasons.

However, from August 12th we had a week of heavenly weather; real harvest weather, with blue cloudless skies and intense heat. The uncut wheat was so ripe it was deep brown in colour – a rich deep brown which looked glowing backed by a belt of dark trees and vivid blue sky above. All our energies were set to get it in as quickly as possible and one of the nicest things about harvesting is the sense of enthusiasm and camaraderie in the harvest fields in fine weather. There is no-one who grudges his labour. Even the gypsies put their backs into it and work tirelessly and with real vim. There were colourful groups working at the Park – the gypsies with their usual gay assortment of colours, South American[70] soldiers who shed their khaki coats, displaying blue-black, brown-black and grey-black arms – and a band of little boy scouts with bright green ties and kerchiefs and old Joe in his white hat.

Dorothy and I cut the first wheat with the new reaper and binder; a lovely machine whose wings were painted the same colour as the corn. It was blistering hot on the tractor and the hot air danced over the field dazzling one's eyes. But what a fascinating job driving round and round this great golden field each turn reducing the margin of tender green. Fascinating it was to watch the lathes fall quickly on the platform, being swung up the canvas rollers and shot out in bundles on to the stubble. As we went round, groups of tireless workers followed "stooking up", so that by the time we had made a turn, our way was left clear and green.

Day after day we worked thus, Dorothy and I, driving in turns and sitting on the binders watching that all went well. Day after day in scorching sun, till at last it began to set, casting long peaceful shadows across the fields about 9 o'clock each evening.

I think we all felt that every ounce of energy we had, we must expand. I have never seen work done so vigorously or so generously. This was our small part in the war effort. Our armies were winning their way to victory and this was our share and our gratitude. Even when it rained, we felt we could not grumble because the war was going so well.

Our troops swept across the continent with simply breathtaking speed. Every day came news of fresh advances. On September 4th we entered Belgium, on September 5th we entered Holland. All the old names of the last war were being mentioned. Pictures came through of Monty standing at Vimy Ridge[71] and this seemed to thrill the old veterans more than anything. The Americans swept on towards the Ziegfried Line[72] and forced a wedge into Germany. The Fifth Army made a brilliant breakthrough on the Adriatic side of the Gothic Line with every indication that the Huns would soon be chased out of Italy. Bulgaria and Romania declared war against Germany and last, but not least, we had captured every flying bomb base and the papers announced "the end of the Buzz Bomb"[73] Blackout restrictions were ordered to be relaxed. There were to be lighting in the streets again and only light curtains were now necessary.

Surely there was every hope of peace before the winter? No alerts! No blackout! When would it finish? Some said weeks, some months. Anyway, it could not be long now and we could put all our energy into this last lap, here on the Home Front.

We cleared fields of corn and as soon as they were clear, we got busy with the two tractors discing and ploughing and then seeding. (It is important to plough in the fresh stubble as soon as possible).

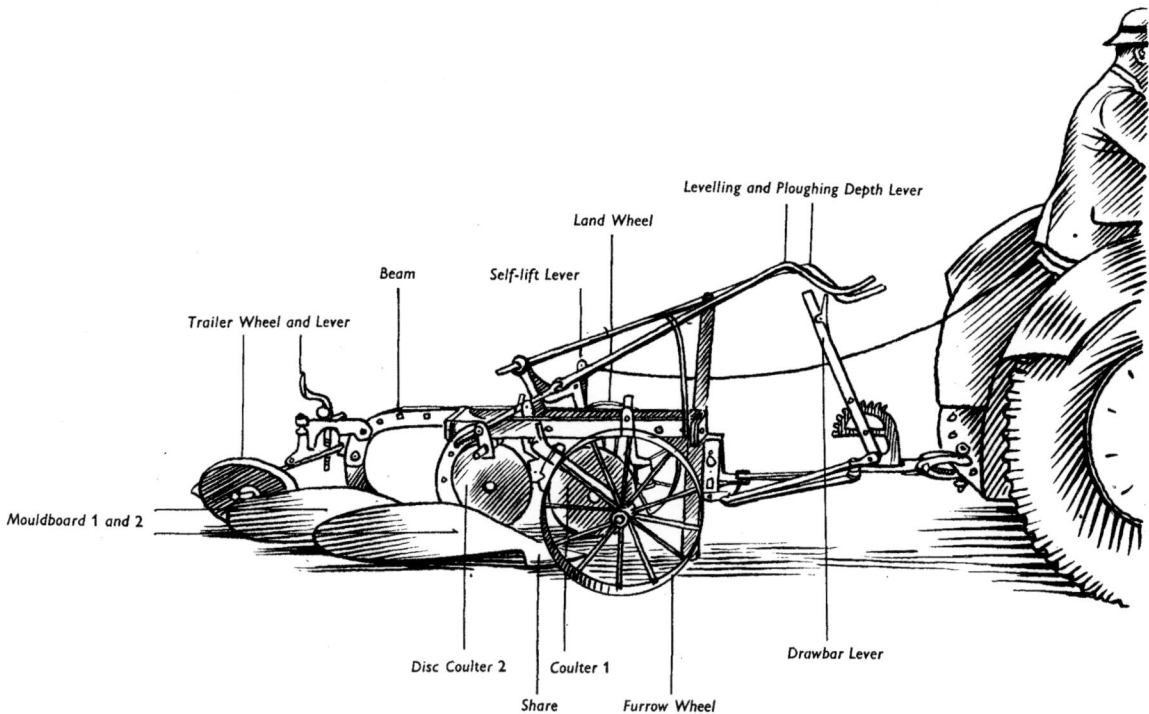

TWO FURROW TRACTOR PLOUGH

Ploughing by the book. Evelyn Dunbar's intricate drawing of a two furrow tractor plough comes from *A Book of Farmcraft*. Learning to plough, Anne found, was down to advice and practice, rather than book learning.

My greatest pleasure was cutting the 30 acre fields which I had sown in mid-March. This was exactly the same sort of day. Then full of the promise of spring, now autumn, with hot sun and a bright clear air. The field stretches over the highest ground at the Park, which affords a fine view and makes you feel on top of the world. It was thrilling to be cutting my oats – a thing I had hoped I should be here to as A. G. Street writes "To go away and not see my first crop would have been the act of a traitor."[74] My first crop was a poor crop but I still felt proud of it as I went round and round that great field hour after hour. For 8 hours, I sat on the tractor without a stop, watching the light swathes falling ever backwards, snipping off sharp corners and swinging round smooth bends, wending my way about groups of great parkland trees who made my cutting into a pattern of intricate shape.

OATS

Identifying different crops was something newcomers to the soil needed to learn, and in *A Book of Farmcraft* Evelyn Dunbar illustrates wheat, barley and oats with this in mind.

The oats being short and thin, there was no need for anyone to sit on the binder. I was glad of this because I prefer to work alone long hours. "Silence, solitude and contemplation are the fundamental constituents of farming life and, I would add, of country life altogether" (Sir George Stapledon)[75]

I think it took me 3 days to get the field "down." The Boss came along just as I was sweeping through the last tiny strip which stood up like the last fringe of hair on a man's bald head. Snip! snip! snip! It was flat. "The last cut of this season," the Boss remarked as he showed me where to take the tractor and how to fold up the binder ready for its journey farmwards. He left me to drive home for his supper and regretfully I loosened the rollers and the canvas and piled empty sacks and oil tins on the platform. Regretfully, because I knew that this would probably be the last time in my life when I should cut corn. It had been an enriching experience and somehow now it seemed as if I had come to the end of this chapter. Walter writes "The harvest is the goal to which the main efforts of the past year have been directed" and I felt that this was the goal to which my farming efforts of the past year had been directed. I had suddenly acquired the confidence of knowing that I knew my job. I knew now what must be done and more or less how to do it. I could think things out for myself and offer suggestions. I could take the responsibility of my own decisions and I knew that I could tackle any job that came my way with efficiency and a certain amount of ease. At last, I was a useful member of this community and now I must soon leave it. I regretted that, but with what joy I looked forward to the gathering up of the old threads of home life, to love and companionship and leisure which, of necessity, I had forgotten, had not dared to think about. I had given my whole self to my work and found great happiness, but not complete happiness. A life a thousand times richer and a thousand times more complete lay ahead. It would not be long to wait now and when it came, I should remember with gratitude that I had reached my goal, that I had sown and reaped and gathered in a fragment of England's Harvest.

Peter Plays Truant

It was with a certain feeling of relaxation that I went onto the milk round again. My month on the farm had stretched itself almost into two. Twice I had sallied forth to relieve Barbara and twice been reprieved. First for harvesting and again for threshing. "I don't want to turn your head, Anne, but you're too useful on the farm," said the Boss and I felt highly flattered because this was the first compliment he had ever paid me. I had often longed for a word of praise, even angled for it, till I realised it was not his way. He was like Mrs Lippet "Ye didn't expect fer me ter praise 'ee surely. 'Twouldn't be natural. Praise do make young folk uppish" (Farmer's Glory[76]). It didn't make me uppish, at least I didn't think so, but it made me warm and happy and determined to be more than ever useful on the farm.

The sad thing about the round was that Peter was lost. On September 2nd, he ran loose with a crowd of forest ponies who broke down the fences of his field and careered away.

New Forest ponies are not tame creatures. Peter, the somewhat wayward pony at New Park Farm, disappeared when he was tempted to go off with a bunch of wild ponies. The saga unfolds over several pages of the diary.
Photograph by Graham Cooper.

We were so busy that no-one really could be spared to go and hunt for him. "He'll wander back" they all said and Barbara took old Brownie in his stead and day after day I watched for him to return. How I longed for a sight of his dear grey nose. My anxiety grew till one Sunday evening I got a pony from old Mr Dukes and rode the forest hoping to see Peter. My pony, Tommy, was a fresh four year old, who gave me a lot of fun and I enjoyed my ride although my quest was fruitless. Everyone I saw I begged them to look out for Peter. The Boss got in touch with the Foresters[77], who were confident they would find him because of his shod hooves, but still we heard nothing. And then at last, on September 16th, the phone rang. A pony, black with a grey nose, had walked into the Grand Hotel Riding Stables at Lyndhurst. Evidently Peter had decided to be a riding pony instead of a milk pony! It was Saturday and I rushed through my morning's work to get to Lyndhurst in my lunch hour and ride him back. Darling Peter! He had come back just in time to do the round with me on Monday. I knew he would! I was in high exultation and stumped off with saddle and bridle to "hitch-hike" my way to Lyndhurst, which I did most successfully.

The aptly-named Grand Hotel at Lyndhurst

"But when I got there, the cupboard was bare!" As I looked into every loose-box, my heart sank. Some were empty. In some were brown ponies, in some grey ponies, but nowhere was Peter. At last, I saw a girl walking out of the harness room. "He's not here now", she said "I don't know where he is. You'd better go to the Fox and Hounds and ask Ivy. She'd be there". So off I went, very impatiently, because I was longing to see Peter and entered the bar of the Fox and Hounds. It was 12 o'clock and thick with blue smoke and crowded with the locals drinking their lunchtime pints, all laughing and chatting till I entered, a strange figure in dirty old farm shorts, orange stockings and red scarf and a long green twig which I had brought in place of a riding crop. "Is there anyone here called Ivy?" I asked, trying my best to assume a casual air. "Yes", she said, stepping forward, immaculate in smart tweed jacket and jodhpurs. She was drinking a beer with her Groom. "Oh! The pony with the grey nose", she said "he was turned out onto the Bench[78] this morning with the others. You'll be likely to find him if you go and look". I was speechless with horror and anger. How could they turn him out. We might never find him again now.

The groom came down the road with me and set me on my way with a bowl of oats and a halter, telling me about Peter and how nervous he was. "Never seen such a timid pony" he said "wouldn't let me near him – a bundle of nerves he was, but you'll find him all right, never fear. And if you don't, he'll come in tonight with the others and I'll keep him for you in the morning." But I didn't find him, although I trudged for miles over the Bench and far along the forest. And he didn't come in with the others that night and on Monday I had to take old Brownie, who is so slow I can hardly bear it. She adds quite an hour onto my round and wears me out with impatience. I'd feel less tired doing the round three times over with Peter. How I long for him to come back.

About 3 days later, market day at Salisbury, the phone rang. Everyone was out, so I answered it and found myself speaking to the Head Agister[79] who gave me wonderful news. Peter was in the stable-yard of the Beaulieu Road Station Hotel and would someone go and fetch him.

A small woodcut by Anne, which she and her husband used as their book plate. They felt life was a voyage of discovery: each day you should go forth to seek. Anne usually persisted when she set her mind to do something – even if it was searching for a missing pony.

Beaulieu Road Station Hotel in the 1940s.

"Of course" I said but when I discussed how with Joe, he put every obstacle in my way. Beaulieu Road Station is about 4 miles the other side of Lyndhurst across the high moorland. There are no buses, probably no cars to hitchhike with and probably no taxi would take me. If I went on my bike, how could I get it home? And how get the saddle and bridle there? And if I didn't, would it be too late to go after work before blackout and I should get lost in the forest. He elaborated all the terrible things that might happen and, seeing my determination unbroken, he resorted to sarcasm and said bitingly "You're not the only bloke on the farm you know. There's plenty of others who can fetch him tomorrow". But tomorrow was my day off and I wanted to fetch him tonight and seeing that Joe was in no mood to be argued with, I held my peace and milked the cows demurely thinking the while how it could be done. Luckily, we finished in good time and old Joe wandered off to his cottage, waving his hand and saying "Have a good day tomorrow Anne, and I'll promise you your darling Peter'll be in the field waiting for you on Friday." The minute he'd disappeared, I tied my saddle and bridle onto the back of my bike and was off and pedalled as I've never pedalled in my life before, till I reached Beaulieu Road Station Hotel at 6 o'clock. "Mine Host", a fat, round-bellied monster, with a mop of curly hair and not a tooth in his head, but cheerful withal, greeted me and opened a garage door, revealing Peter standing within. How delighted he was to see me. It was a joyful reunion. He rubbed his nose round and round my chest and gave little snorts of rapture and gobbled up the bagfuls of oats I had brought for him and rubbed his nose all over me again. I cut a stick and rode away, leaving my bike to fetch tomorrow. It was a gorgeous ride on a wonderful evening with the sun just setting across the wide open moor, coloured with "spoiling" bracken. The air was cool and Peter was fresh after his long rest. I was wearing my farm shorts and liked the grip of the saddle on my bare knees and the cold air blowing over my legs. This was grand. What I had wanted to do ever since I came, to ride Peter, and it was far better than I imagined. We knew each other so perfectly and were in complete unison and being on his back was so much better than being in the float. We raced along and each time I spoke to him his ears pricked and he gave little snorts of pleasure. All along the chalky soil, on the high ridge of moorland we cantered. Flat out, like a streak in wonderful harmony. I sensed his joy at being no longer lost and lonely and that eight miles home was rapturous. We turned into New Park at 6.45pm, well before dusk and as we clattered past Joe's cottage, there he was feeding his pig. He looked in amazement and only said "So you've got him Anne," but I could see by the smile in his eyes that he was amused and appreciative and bore me no grudge for disobeying him so flagrantly.

Next day, I took the train to fetch my bike, another glorious day, and struck home through the forest which stretched for miles like Malayan jungle. I couldn't feel that it was either interesting or beautiful and I wondered exactly why it has been preserved for so long. I felt that hundreds of trees could be spared with positive advantage and yet if anyone dared to suggest it, there would be great protest. I could imagine early Britain smothered in forest like this and how grateful the earth must have been to feel her bosom bared to the sun and wind.

October

Threshing following after the harvest, but except for being rather more than usually shorthanded at milking times, this did not affect me as I was either on the round or the farm. The War Agricultural[80] did our threshing and they brought their own band of girls, who must be a very tough crowd, threshing all day, month-in month-out. The boys and old Jack helped them – Jack building the ricks and the Boss supervising. He was pleased to find that the wheat was not as much spoilt by the rain as he had expected. We got over 200 sacks. But the oats were a miserable yield, scarcely worth the threshing. We just got a little more than we put in, which only averaged 2 sacks to the acre.

We all breathed a sigh of relief when this job was done, for now we could arrange our annual holidays – a week each. Dorothy took hers first and spent it at Bournemouth and the minute she came back I gleefully packed my bag for Scotland. I had a heavenly "leave" which started the minute I entered the train and sat on my bag in the corridor, just ruminating. There followed a series of breakfasts-in-bed and lovely meals and gossip, and sitting knitting by the fire. It was an added luxury when I slept in my niece's now disused nursery to waken and find a group of cows walking round the frieze and know there was no need to milk them! I felt really relaxed and ready to tackle the winter when the time came for me to return. I cycled back to the farm at midday; a mild November day with bright warm sun. The old buildings and the great oaks in sweeping sun-swept pastures seemed so mellow and familiar after the sterner face of Scotland and there even was the Boss and the girls with Polly, the new pony, in the coach yard. All such friendly, familiar faces as if they had been there ever since I left. I said "Well I've travelled about 500 miles since I saw you, but I haven't seen anywhere as lovely as this." And I hadn't.

Freda left next day for her holiday and then the fun began. Dorothy and Barbara were on the milk rounds and I was left on the farm in charge of the calves and dairy – and Barbara got ill. We were anxious not to recall Freda but we were indeed in a jam. The only way out I could think of was to give the furthest away North Weirs[81] customers enough milk to last 2 days. I thought it out as I drove along and decided anyway to try it. I left a series of little notes to this effect with every bottle where I could find no-one to explain the reason why. Most people were very understanding and agreed that so long as the milk kept, it didn't matter. It eased the situation at the farm considerably and cut down my round by about an hour and a half a day, so that I was able to do the calves and be back in time for milking. In fact it was such a success from our point of view that when Barbara came back, the Boss told us to carry on like this for the winter. We of course were delighted because the wind and the rain sweeping across the weirs in winter is no fun but a few of our customers grew a little restive when they realised it was to be a permanency.

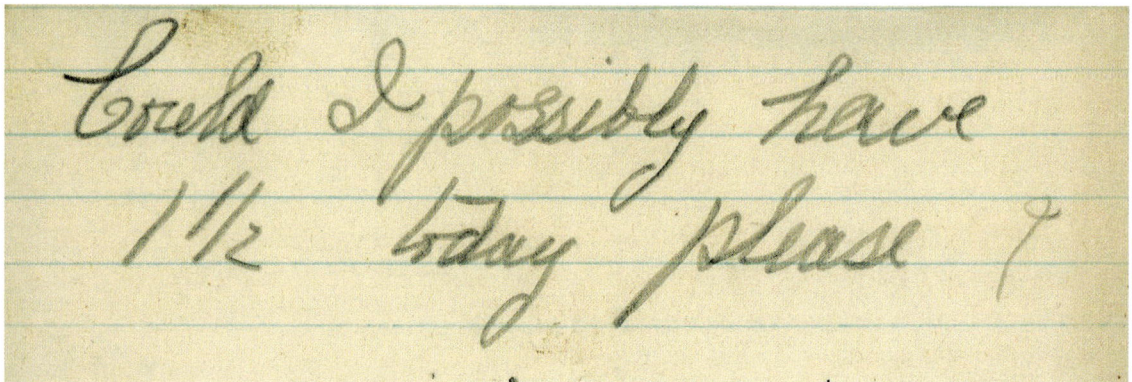

A doorstep note as brief as it is polite. The customer who wrote it would undoubtedly be astonished that *The Milk Lady at New Park Farm* pocketed it as a memento.

However, to keep them sweet, we gave them a drop extra and the grumbles soon subsided except for a certain Mrs Gulliver, who raised Cain! We told her that if she wanted her milk every day, we'd leave it in the village and her husband could bring it home from work. She stormed and said that we girls were paid to take the milk to her door and she'd have it every day at her door if the King of England had to bring it. Like several others, she blamed it entirely on our laziness and failed to appreciate the shortness of labour in wartime. We have advertised again and again for a girl with no result and the Land Army cannot produce one because they all refuse to do the milk round. However, the Boss stuck to his guns and dealt most skilfully with the husband who was sent up to the farm to make a row. And the upshot was that the Food Office agreed to allow them to change their dairy and now they don't get their milk till half past six in the evening and have to fetch it from the end of the road. So we feel that they have jumped out of the frying pan into the fire and we have just got a new customer who is certainly more agreeable and needs more milk, so that cancels our loss!

November

On November 16th, we did our first winter ploughing after weeks of rain, not "Welcome waterspouts of blessed rain[82]" but soggy downpours that kept us off the fields and turned on the lights almost at midday. Day after day on the milk round, I would wear a double-lined fishing mackintosh, a Harris Tweed jacket, a Fair Isle jersey and a shirt and long before I was home, the rain would be well through them all. It seemed that we could never get down to our ploughing, or sow our winter wheat. The ground was simply waterlogged with the stubble, soft and rotted. However at last, the Boss thought he might have a try and I went to take over in the lunch hour. A damp wind was sweeping across the Kennel field where we were working and I was delighted to feel the throb of the tractor once more, steering my course over what was little more than a sea of mud. Gulls and starlings hungrily followed in my wake, screaming greedily for their long postponed feast. Once more, I became gripped by the spell which tractor work always gives me – that I want to go on and on and on! How I hoped the Boss would delay his lunch hour so that I might continue as long as possible.

A. G. Street writes that ploughing is "the most charming disguise work can wear."[83] He says "As you become intimate with it, you find that you have ceased to be the operation of a mere farm implement. You and the plough have become one, a common intelligence with one idea only – to plough on and on and on. Your mind stands calmly aloof, rejoicing in a thing in which it has no conscious part, noting with a detached satisfaction the perfect furrow, which falls away on your right in an infinite ribbon." I have watched the War Agricultural ploughing the rough moorland virgin land, and I can appreciate what he says about ploughing Virgin Land – "If ploughing generally be conceded a pleasing thing to do, then to plough virgin land is pure joy. The thought that you are ploughing the land for the first time since the world began satisfies your innermost soul. Each furrow is such a definite little stride in the world's history." What I also rejoice in is the transforming effect it has on the landscape – rich bands of deep brown soil appearing over large areas of pale stubble and widening each day until the whole is one uniform colour. The beauty of the scenery around me is a great part of the joy that I get out of my work. I am forever conscious of it and I absorb it, so that I am now able to recall visually any work I have done over nearly two years. My mind is a kaleidoscope of scenes in spring, summer, autumn and winter as the crops and the colours have changed. I have a wealth of memories which I hope I shall keep for always.

But ploughing today was much hindered by the mud. I was armed with a great spade and was forced continually to stop to dig myself out and untwine a mass of weeds from the wheels and blades. We were using the new 2-furrow plough which was heavier and sunk in deeper than the old one and the Boss agreed it was rather impossible, so we packed up and left it, little realising how long it would be before we should have a chance to carry on again. The rain continued till Christmas and was followed by severe frosts which froze the ground like iron. We had to go on waiting with never a seed of winter wheat in the ground, which should have been sown in October. This was the only time I have ever seen the Boss show any impatience, for he was not fully occupied and he was longing to be busy.

Christmas 1944

Christmas came round again with the usual feeling of excitement and hustle and good cheer. Everybody was making presents and buying presents and sending cards overseas in the joyful hope and calm assumption that this anyway would be the last wartime Christmas. "A peaceful one next year" was on every lip and great preparations were made to have it as gay as possible. Wishful thinkers, all of us, like the man in the Daily Mail cartoon who pinned a large notice on to his stocking which read 'Dear Santa, I would like a nice stocking full of peace'. He had a rude awakening indeed when a horrid Nazi jumped out of Santa's sack and punched him one on the nose. And so had we, when only a few days before Christmas we found that the enemy had launched a terrific counter attack on the American lines, were advancing rapidly and already claiming that they would reach Paris by Christmas. The atmosphere was tense. The Christmas spirit dissolved in one night, but people mechanically kept on making plum puddings and mince pies and icing large cakes over a thick coating of synthetic almond paste. I watched them in every kitchen as I left the milk and not a soul spoke of the war. I had arranged a small Christmas tree with evergreens and painted apples and silver anti-location paper[84] which the Huns had dropped in our fields in the summer. It almost seemed to mock me now and yet something compelled me to keep it there and to string my Christmas cards across the room and I was glad I did so because I chanced to entertain a young Canadian pilot, just over here one week, and gave him a cracker from my tree, which came from Toronto, his home town, and lemons and dried fruits from Italy. Somehow the old spirit of Christmas forces itself even in the darkest days and this year the weather certainly helped. Weeks, I should say, months of rain suddenly changed on Christmas Eve to hard white frost, transforming the countryside into a Dickensian scene. The sun shone in a blue cloudless sky and at night the moon was like a great yellow ball. It was impossible to feel so gloomy on days like this. Our spirits rose willy nilly and although news from the western front[85] was withheld, we anyway felt more optimistic.

At the farm, we had the usual preparations of laying in a store of logs and hay and roots. Again, I went hay-carting and experienced that most wonderful of all sensations of lying on top of the load as we brought it home. "It is doubtful if the luxury can be equalled . . . . It is a short surrender to perfect ease, a glad yielding to a swaying movement with only the blue sky . . . above . . . ." (Walter Rose).

Around Christmas time, not long before she left New Park, Anne goes hay-carting again bringing in fodder for the cows. She finds an undiminished pleasure in one aspect of this job. "At the farm," she writes, "we had the usual preparations of laying in a store of logs and hay and roots. Again, I went hay-carting and experienced that most wonderful of all sensations of lying on top of the load as we brought it home." Evelyn Dunbar catches the spirit of that sensation in this tiny drawing in *A Book of Farmcraft*.

I shall never forget the exquisite joy of it last year on Christmas Eve, on a day similar to this, except that the sky then was piled high with mountains of white clouds which became pink tipped in the late afternoon. I was glad to find that my memory of this sensation had not increased in my imagination. It was equally pleasant this year.

I promised to do the milk round the whole of Christmas, partly because Barbara expected her Bill home on leave and partly because I would rather be working than having time off. My only worry was the question of milk as we had had bad luck this month. Old Dilly, our Number One cow had contracted milk fever when her calf was born and she was found dead in the cowshed the next morning. It was a great loss. She was a fine 6 gallon cow and we had been relying on her for our winter milk supply. Clover calved a few days later, so for a while, we were all right, but one morning, she also was found lying dead in the ditch of the Ley field. The cows had hooked her there and unable to rise she had frozen to death. I asked the Boss the meaning of this and he explained that in the winter when the fields are bare, the cows, having nothing better to do, start quarrelling and when one is hooked, all the others set on her, like idle people who generally end up by having a row. So it looked as if we were to be really short of milk for Christmas and almost every house had at least one visitor, or "a boy," coming home on leave. Some had 3 or 4. I felt depressed beyond words at the prospect of being short and having to say no at Christmas time. However the Boss just saved the situation in his usual quick way by buying a cow at Salisbury 3 days before Christmas. He brought her home in triumph and said "I've really bought a cow for you at last. She's come from Scotland and she must be called Anne." She was a great, strong, wild-looking creature with an immense head and heavy jowl and close curling hair, an Ayrshire with pointed spreading horns and round, fierce bull-like eyes. She guarded her calf with true Scots determination and would return again and again to the cowshed lowing, instead of going up the lane with the rest. I was proud of her. I thought her a marvellous creature. In my eyes she dwarfed the rest of the herd and I felt that Scotland had really shown England a thing or two.

She certainly saved the situation as far as milk was concerned and I had ample to dish out to all my emergency customers over Christmas, for which I was truly grateful.

Christmas morning was an unusually early one. We were all vigorous in our matutinal duties and there was much ribaldry in the exchange of gifts. Peter, my pony, sent me a lovely pair of stockings which he had chosen for me in London and a little powder pot, which caused great fun as old Joe is forever teasing me and saying that Peter doesn't really love me and now I say I have proof that he does!

I set off nice and early on the round, Peter looking festive with holly and mistletoe twined in his bridle and his brasses specially bright. My memory of the round is a succession of drinks beginning with an immense double rum at the Rose and Crown and followed there after by countless sherries, ports and gins with huge chunks of Christmas cake and mince pies. I just sailed along blissfully. With never a bite of breakfast, in the intense frosty air it is a wonder I survived at all. I never felt a bump in the road and was conscious that Peter was trotting unusually fast. I relied on him entirely to stop when he should and he did. I was showered with gifts all the way. Cigarettes, soap, tea, a handkerchief, a plum pudding, a Christmas cake, egg cosies, pork chops, Brussels sprouts, carrots, onions, chocolate biscuits, eggs and 2 cured rabbit skins and 2 presents of money. People were a little diffident about "tipping" me, so the ones who really wanted to give me something gave me presents and the others had a good excuse! Barbara came home very amused one day because one old cottager had pressed half a crown into her hand and then said "Anne is a lady, isn't she?" Barbara, not quite knowing what to say, supposed she'd better say yes and the old dame replied, "Yes, you can see she's a lady" then feeling she might have offended Barbara's feelings added: "Not that I mean any offence to you. What we'll say is that Anne is a lady, but you and I aren't!"

The Rose and Crown, Brockenhurst. The pub is on the Lyndhurst road.

The Boss was much amused at this story and recounted it with gusto to Joe when we were milking. He said "What do you think Joe? I say, perhaps she was once!" Whereupon Joe, as quick as a flash, replied stoutly, "I say she is because this morning when Peter bit her, she didn't cry out or scream, she just said quite quietly 'Joe, Peter's bitten me' and when I asked her where, she said 'I can't tell you'. So I think she is a lady!" I am always amazed at the quickness and depths of Joe's wit and I think this is a good example. Another occasion when he excelled himself was one day when, instead of slipping my most treasured watch from Italy into my pocket, I dropped it down inside my breeches and it fell to my knee. That time, I confess, I did scream because I thought it had fallen to the ground. Joe looked round quizzically out of the corner of his eye and remarked "I hope it is SHOCKPROOF"! – surely a brilliant remark and most surprising from someone seemingly so stolid and so simple.

My short round, which I had meant to whiz round on Christmas morning, proved unbelievably lengthy. For, as well as drinking my many drinks and eating my cakes and pies and receiving my gifts, I had also to inspect all the Christmas trees and see what the children had found in their stockings and by this time I was in no mood to hurry about anything. But at last, Peter's head was turned farmwards and at last we clattered into the coach yard. The cows were already in the sheds, tied up, and the boys as merry on beer as myself on my mixture. Old Jack helped me to unharness and then we started milking. We chattered and sang songs till we got to the top of the first shed and then we became stone cold sober. Fred sat under Anne, the new Ayrshire. Whether she was missing her calf, who was weaned the day before, or whether her Scots prejudice rebelled against alcohol, I know not. Anyway, she biffed Fred one in the middle and tossed him headlong down the gutter, taking a leg clean off his stool. Fred refused to go near her again and the others also, and Jack said, "Anne'll milk her. She often does" and my pride being tickled I felt quite fearless and retorted "I'll milk her and if she kicks me, I'll knock her block off!" I was just stooping down to wipe her off when she landed me a terrific crippling blow on the knee and followed with six more, quick as lightning from the middle of my calf to the top of my thigh and I was in such pain I just stood rooted to the spot, unable to move. It was agony and I had to revive myself with a drink of very cold water, but I laughed when I thought of my bravado declaring that I would "knock her block off". I've never been near her since. My marvellous Scotch namesake! She can go back to Scotland for all I care. No-one will milk her except Joe and he will only do her standing up, with two ropes on. She jumps sideways and kicks at the same time and has nearly landed Joe on his back several times. The spiteful brute. I shiver even to look at her.

We finished nice and early that afternoon and I followed on with a sherry party first and then the jolliest of dinner parties with goose and plum pudding and good Madeira, which soothed away the pain in my leg and ended Christmas on a high note. Friends have been so kind inviting me out so that I should not feel lonely. I had quite a dozen invitations for Christmas dinner. Two people I have never even met and I don't even know by sight asked me to join them, but my perplexity now when I do the round is to wonder who they are, so I give a gratifying grin to everyone and hope they are included.

Boxing Day brought the usual reactions. Most people stayed indoors feeling slightly depressed and livery. I refused the few drinks I was offered. Christmas was over and they seemed out of place now. I was ready to get back to my routine. It had been a good Christmas but I was glad it was over.

Farmer's Brains Trust

For some reason best known to themselves, the Daily Express decided to stage a Farmer's Brains Trust at Brockenhurst. Several of the BBC Brains Trusters were here, with Commander Campbell as Question Master. Lord Winster, Sir Cleveland Fyfe, Frederick Allen ("this is the news and Frederick Allen reading it!") and two local farmers, Tom Parker and George Blomfield, the first a successful farmer of some 2,000 acres, which he had acquired by his own efforts and the latter a smallholder. The village hall[86] was all laid out with imposing placards on the platform and a microphone for each speaker. It was quite exciting! We had been invited to send in questions and I sent in one and the Boss sent four. They answered my one and one of his on ley farming. It was amusing to see the two ruddy-faced and very blunt spoken countrymen sitting with the highly immaculate city Brains Trusters! But they were both characters and I should say the life and the soul of the whole party.

I was thrilled when Cdre Campbell read out my question, of course getting himself all tied up with the pronunciation of my name, which provoked a dig in the ribs from the Boss and a grin from all my friends! I asked whether the modern farmer who travels about the country in his car and who has the distractions of the cinema etc., is as good a farmer, or farm hand, as the man of 100 years ago who devoted his whole life to his land? Unfortunately, they made it sound rather priggish, as if I thought he shouldn't go to the cinema! I had thought it would provoke a good argument, but there was just no discussion because they, one and all, unanimously agreed that the modern farmer is undoubtedly the best this country has ever seen! They said he produced more per acre than ever before and that the mechanisation of the land has enabled him to have leisure which he needs and, equally important, leisure to take his wife about. They said that in the old days, the farmer was nothing more than a drudge and his wife also. Still I am not convinced because I think the old farmer was a craftsman and he went on working because he loved it. The village policeman definitely does not agree. He says "Why, just look at their fences. In the old days, they would carpenter new posts and rebuild them solid. Now they just twine a bit of wire round them and hope for the best!"

On the whole, I decided that the Brains Trust doesn't really answer any question very satisfactorily. They banter and hurl rude, amusing remarks at each other, but they don't really get down to it. So much more could have been made of so many interesting questions, such as the Nationalisation of the Land, the effect of intensive milk production etc., but it is not till you get home that you realise you have been left high and dry and then you begin to feel annoyed!

The meeting ended with the last question "What are the qualities of a good farmer?" Lord Winster promptly replied: "Patience, the patience of Job." Sir Cleveland Fyfe added "Courage" and Frederick Allen "a love of the land and a desire to serve it". Tom Parker, the Fareham farmer, spoke up in his broad Hampshire drawl: "I don't know what he should be, but I know what he should do. He should be able to sow every one of his fields so that it comes up full and he should be able to stand on his land blindfold and know what to put there next year."

Old man Knapp, in the audience, stood up and told us that his father had a family of 8 sons and 7 daughters and they all worked on his farm and in his opinion, any man who wanted to be a good farmer should first of all raise a good family – and choose the right wife!

Another New Year – 1945

"When icicles hang on the wall
And Dick the Shepherd blows his nail
And Tom bears logs into the hall
And milk comes frozen home in pail[87]"

Milk was frozen in pail with a vengeance. Hard frosts held on into the New Year, the most severe since 1890 the papers said. But they were really glorious days, the first week or so – bright and crisp and energising, with roads as dry as bone, so that Peter's hooves made a lovely clipperty clopperty noise in the still air as he trotted along with his head held high, obviously enjoying it too. But certainly it was cold. The milk froze all round my pail in thick chunks of ice cream and I had constantly to thaw the tap of my churn. The milk in the bottles formed one solid block, rose right out of the necks about an inch, pushing the little carton tops up too, where they perched ridiculously, like top-knots on a vol-au-vent. The milk round was bitterly cold in the early morning, but later, when the sun came out, it was lovely. I managed to keep warm thanks to my husband, for I had borrowed his undies. The Boss laughed when I told him. He said he'd heard of a wife wearing the breeches, but never the pants!

Then came the snow. It had been swirling all round us for days and we hoped we might escape, for it is what we dread most. The animals have to be brought in to sleep and fed indoors, masses of straw carted to bed them down and loads of hay and roots cut every day to feed them. All this in addition to the difficulty of getting the horses about on snow-laden ground. We drove the young heifers back from the Park in preparation and found two frozen dead in a pond where they had gone for water and two who were very weak and had to be brought home in the trailer and treated with great care. Luckily they recovered. When the snow did come, it came with a vengeance. I wakened to find it a good six inches deep on the roads and much deeper in the drifts. At this early hour, there had been no traffic on the roads and it was impossible to cycle, so I had to walk the 3½ miles to the farm. I didn't hurry because I knew I should need all my energies for the day ahead, taking Peter along these roads. A pale yellow moon hung in a grey, still snow-laden sky, which made it just possible to discern the line of the road.

We took out the ponies well "roughed," but even so they collected large iceballs in their hooves which we had continually to whack out with a hook. It was hard going for them and for us, driving with a tight rein and staggering up snowy paths with our heavy cans and more perilous still after days of sun which thawed the snow and frost at night, which formed an icy surface again. For miles we had to lead them where it simply was not safe to drive, where we could scarcely keep our own feet and watched their hooves slipping each time they put them to the ground. Peter was simply gallant! He plodded on heroically and relied on my every word for his guidance. I tied a mackintosh over his back to keep the cold out and carried bits of cake to cheer him up from time to time. We also were regaled with cups of hot tea, coffee and cocoa. Most people were amazed to see us at all and said we were real heroes and deserved medals and were so appreciative that we felt the effort was really worthwhile. But we were whacked when we got back to the farm, sometimes as much as two hours late. Freda was my partner in crime and each day we said we couldn't "stick much more." We ached in every limb and my leg, which had a double pony kick added to my six cow bruises of Christmas Day, was really agonising, lifting it over the snow and up and down the float. My long round every other day was just about as much as I could manage. Freda took Henry with her because she had slipped once and felt nervous. I knew I could handle Peter better by myself so I went alone.

Snow and frost – frost registering 27 degrees in the village – lasted about 10 days. The forest looked superb, clad in her mantle of white, so thick that even the strongest evergreens were bowed down. Virgin snow stretched on every side glimmering in the sunlight. It was a real fairyland of beauty. An unreal world of stillness and a queer silence, where no accustomed sound was heard. Even the pony and the float moved soundlessly through the snow and no birds sang[88].

"Sunset at East Boldre." Ten days of bitter frost and disruptively deep snow in January 1945, is followed, to Anne's great relief, by a thaw. Photograph by Jo Holmes / New Forest National Park Authority.

There was obviously a feline thief in the area!

On January 31st, when the moon was at the full and directly opposite the sun, the thaw came at last. Old man Gulliver said it would. We felt the change at midday and by next morning it had really set in. What a blessed relief! My every limb felt relaxed, my mind suddenly calm. Everywhere was the sound of drip, drip – water dropping from the trees, the roofs, the gutters, the thawing pipes. Movement and sound had returned with this healing warmth, as it returns to a house once shrouded with sickness, where one can once more laugh and talk and feel at ease. Birds in every tree twittered and sang for joy, a host of voices raising their Te Deum, sadly depleted I am afraid, for I found many little bodies stretched stiff and cold in the snow. One early morning, a tiny "Polly Wagtail" flew into the cowshed and rested with its claws actually clinging onto the bars of Joe's hurricane lamp for warmth. It stayed there until the lamp had to be removed. I hope it survived.

Gradually the trees became bare again, the fields green and a welcome rain washed the roads clean and smooth. Roofs shot great avalanches of snow down onto the pathways, one right over my back as I bent over my can, dishing out the milk. My customer was just inside her doorway, so she escaped. It was heavenly to feel warm. I discarded my tweed jacket, said thank you to my husband and discarded his undies and felt a wonderful freedom of movement so lightly clad. But my leg was still very painful and I felt exhausted, so I went to my doctor and he prescribed four days sick leave in which to recover, just doing nothing. I felt I needed it and rejoiced in my unexpected good fortune and tried not to think of the others still working.

This quick drawing of a cat by Anne is from her German trip sketchbook, 1926.

A Further Word

Anne McEntegart: *Lanehead looking towards the Cairn Valley*, oil, 1970s.
This was painted from the hill behind the house. (Private Collection)

Anne ended her diary rather abruptly. It isn't known if she went back to work at the farm later in February or not. She did leave for good in early March. Her husband, Mac, was back in England, sadly invalided out of the Air Force. His return, and the fact that everyone believed the war was in its final stages, were the main reasons Anne handed in her notice to New Park.

Her experiences working at the farm certainly influenced Anne's future life and interests. The home life she longed for in the diary began again, at the end of 1945 – in a Dumfriesshire farmhouse called Lanehead. It had sixty acres of land, with open views across the Cairn Valley. This much-loved place was to be Anne's home for well over thirty years. Here she, Mac and John kept about a hundred hens, a few calves for beef, and grew crops their neighbours helped them harvest. Most importantly, they kept and bred goats. Anne believed goat milk helped Mac in his illness. Anne loved the goats. So milking twice a day and cleaning out the dairy once again became her routine. A friend, Guy Crawford, remembers how impressed he was as a boy by the cleanness of the goats and the dairy. Anne made goat milk ice cream and milkshakes which were very popular with visiting children.

Anne with Peter after his arrival at Lanehead

One of Anne's New Park friends came up to Dumfriesshire by train. He heard Anne's voice on the station platform at Dumfries and whinnied with delight. It was Peter, her favourite and unpredictable black pony with the grey nose. He lived from then on at Lanehead in great style, without question.

Anne, Mac and John with the goats at Lanehead.

From photographs it's clear that it was a happily united family that lived at Lanehead. This lasted for almost a decade after the war. But the stoicism and endurance Anne had learned from country people in the New Forest was something she greatly needed when in 1954 Mac died and then, in 1955, John – who like his father was in the Royal Air Force – was killed in a training accident.

Anne had kept a poem Mac had written during the war:-

Fallen Trees

I stood in London streets and saw
A load of England's noble trees
Felled by the cruel god of war
His lusting appetite to appease.
It brought a vision to my eye
Of ugly scars, where woods had been.
I saddened at this tragedy,
Till thinking deeper I have seen
They also make their sacrifice,
As England's sons who gave their all.
These trees, now fallen, which we miss
Have answered too their country's call.

After these tragic events, Anne travelled abroad a lot, though always returning to Lanehead. For a period she let Lanehead and lived in Paris, resuming her career as an artist. It was in Paris that she and the young Claire Petrenko became friends. They shared a love of English literature. Anne confided in her that after her husband and son died she thought of suicide. She plumbed the depths. But instead, says Claire, she became determined to lead an independent life. Her move to Paris "took great courage." Claire has kept all Anne's letters in a shoebox. "She means a lot to me. She still does." When a letter arrived, her family would exclaim: "It's a letter from 'Anne d'Écosse.' " The affection Claire and her husband felt for Anne led them to name their daughter after her.

Starting to make a name for herself in the French capital, Anne illustrated books for children learning English – just as she had for Malayan children when, newly married in the 1930s, she and Mac had been stationed in

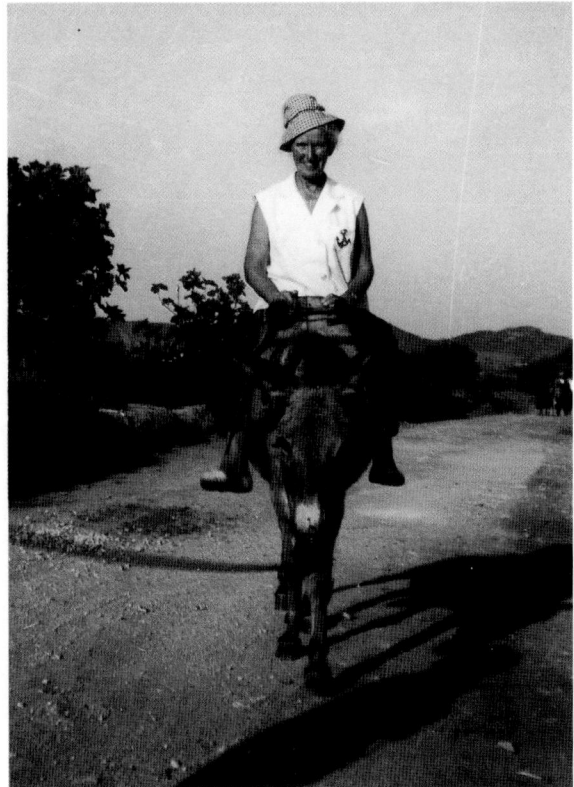

Anne on her travels in Greece

Singapore. For a while in Paris she lived in "two small rooms in a slum" in the suburb of Montreuil. This appealed to her very much. "I should find peace there six stories [sic] high" she noted, "with the sun flooding in." She wrote that these rooms reminded her of the upper room at her lodgings in Brockenhurst where she wrote her diary. She had long found the silence of a simple room appealing, even writing a poem[89] about it in wartime London. Her "pumpkin" was probably a mobile extension of this idea: this was a small, rounded caravan, a symbol of her "independent life." On one of her trips, she drove across the continent, through Italy and Yugoslavia to Greece, and lived all the time in "the pumpkin."

During these travels, she continued to write down her experiences. Once, after she had bought a second-hand typewriter, she described her pleasure in a way that sheds some light on her New Park diary – partly explaining why she wrote it. "It is joyful indeed," she wrote, "that all these thoughts which have been whirling round in my brain may get PUT DOWN ON PAPER AT LAST... Whether anybody reads them or not doesn't really matter, it's GETTING THEM OUT OF MY MIND WHICH IS IMPORTANT."

Anne McEntegart: *Lanehead Pastures – retrospective*, oil, early 1980s. (Private collection)

Anne McEntegart: *Blackface Sheep*, woodcut, 1920s.
Courtesy of Dumfries Museum.

She was a serious and committed artist, though her work is not well known. She worked quietly, without publicity. A traumatic incident in Paris had not helped in this respect. She had prepared a one-woman show, but the night before the opening the vehicle with the paintings in it was stolen. The paintings were never recovered and after this she never attempted to show her work in public again. The artist Peter Doig, in 2007, paid a tribute to his great aunt, Anne McEntegart, describing her as "a real artist." He went on to say "...She was a kind of mythical figure within our family. She made many landscape paintings, etchings, woodcuts, also some sculpture, and had her own press. Her style is hard to describe, other than a kind of Scottish/British post-Impressionism. She was not a sentimental artist."
[*Peter Doig* by Adrian Searle, Kitty Scott, Catherine Grenier, Phaidon (2007)]

Claire is one of many people who continue to treasure Anne's gift for friendship. Her friends remember how sociable she was. They mention long country walks with her infused with talk and laughter. She was a source of almost maternal inspiration and encouragement, particularly to young people. Susan Seright was a child when they first met. She has also kept all Anne's letters. They are "always positive" and they are also funny, bursting with energy, underlinings, sudden emphatic capitals, excited exclamation marks.

By this time, Anne had left Paris for good and was living at Lanehead where she had two studios to work in. But she still went on travelling extensively.

In 1979, after much soul-searching, she decided to move from Lanehead to Appleby-in-Westmorland. This was not so much downsizing as relocating in a town with amenities in easy reach. Nor was she considering retirement. Behind her chosen Georgian house in Appleby was what had been a "dame school." She turned this into a sizeable working studio.

In a letter to Susan explaining her planned move, Anne's relish of this challenge to start again from scratch, is clear. The house "really is a GEM," she writes. It had dry rot, woodworm, rising damp and needed to have some walls pulled down. "I'll be sitting on a pile of rubble for a year at least." Always keen to learn fresh things and have new experiences, it sounds as if Anne could hardly wait. She was extraordinarily resilient. Her zest for life she had once called her "old war horse spirit."

Anne's Georgian house in Appleby-in-Westmorland

Anne and Hebe, her springer spaniel, on a picnic in the late 1970s.

Anne was always an enthusiastic letter writer. She seems likely to have kept in touch with her New Park friends. Roy Fripp, son of "Old Joe" the head cowman at New Park, says that his mother, Olga, "thought the world of Anne" and they corresponded for the rest of their lives.

When she had left Brockenhurst in March 1945, Anne had received three touching letters from there which she kept. They round off the story of The Milk Lady at New Park Farm with grace and affection:-

Letter from Barbara's mother Ethel Carter:

Grey Rock

March 1st 1945

My Dear Mrs Mac

How thrilled I am to learn from Barbara this morning that the wonderful news we heard yesterday is really true, and that so soon you will have "Mr Mac" safely home after his long absence.

I realise how filled with anxiety these years have been and the deep down loneliness you have had to endure, with both your dear ones so far away.

Both Barbara and I have so admired the brave and cheery manner you have somehow managed to maintain against these heavy odds, altho' I simply would not have dared to mention this at any other time; why, it would have felt like stepping upon something sacred.

I must now take this opportunity to say a very big thank you for all the patience and unfailing encouragement you have so readily given to Barbara, for the comradeship she has so enjoyed, and for your grand sense of humour. It has all meant a great deal to my dear, rough and ready, unladylike, untidy daughter.

Hope that these first few flowers (they are all that are "out" yet; wish there were more) will say for me all I would like to say, but cannot.

I wish you all, my dear, all the happiness and luck in the world, for many many years to come,

Yours very sincerely,

Ethel M. Carter

Letter from Barbara Carter:

Grey Rock,

Partridge Rd.,

Brockenhurst,

Hants

8th March 1945

My dear Anne, I was delighted to receive your letter yesterday, and to hear how you were getting on. Please don't worry about us down on the farm we are managing alright, and I am really ever so pleased that Mac is home. Forgive me for calling him Mac but we've always spoken of him by name, and his full address seems so unfriendly. No I didn't laugh I'm sure you alone can help him, and after all who but you should be with him now. It was good of you to invite me on that Sunday morning to see him, he is very nice indeed and [I] really am happy for you both.

You probably think I was pretty dumb on Sunday morning when I left you. I felt rather chocked and was afraid of making a fool of myself. Really Anne I don't know when I felt saying goodbye to anyone so much as I did you, I liked you so very very much and now you've gone the farm seems so empty. I knew how much I would miss you and when I realised that you really were going I did feel full up. Anyhow I am glad you are together again and I do sincerely hope that you will not be separated again and that John will come home to make one happy family.

It is a shame Mac's homecoming was on sick grounds, but he's back in Blighty and after all that's the main factor. Surely with your cheery person about him you will soon make him his old self again.

I told Peter this morning that I'd had a letter from you. He's going to be rather spoilt as I feel I've got to make a fuss of him now his "Mummie" has gone and he's a poor little black orphan. Joe fixed me up with a new collar and traces this morning. Of course the collar broke, Peter walked out of the float and I took one flying leap. It was a long round and I ran out of milk. Eventually we got back, we didn't finish work until about 5.45 pm and just after 6 saw me plodding up Fathers' Field with the cow juice. "What I do for England."

There was a deuce of a row at the farm yesterday. Freda was refused her day off and she took it. Mrs Gossling came out to tell me about it white with rage accompanied by Dorothy very red in the face. It was a lark. Anyhow eventually the day ended. The boss said I would have to do both rounds so I got into a temper and in the end I did mine and tore over to the other round to help Dorothy with that, as she didn't start till about 10.30 am. What a day. The atmosphere was pretty tense today. However I guess it will all work out.

By the way I went with Frank our marine to Careys Manor[90] to their party. I enjoyed it so very much and Frank is a super dancer. Tomorrow we are going to the R.A.F. dance at the Morant Hall.[91] He is splendid company too, but of course he is married.

Well Anne I must close now I guess. In the meantime I shall be wondering how you are faring, and looking forward to hearing from you again. You will be pretty well occupied as a lady, but if you can spare a moment for a poor hard working milk girl, you will I can assure you be making me very happy, as I would hate to lose touch with you.

Before I close I have been asked by many of our customers to be very kindly remembered. Mrs Gulliver and Knott were I could see genuinely upset to think they would not be seeing you.[92]

Happy landings, God bless you both.

Love,

Babs

Letter from Dorothy Gossling:

New Park Farm

Brockenhurst

8th March

Dear Anne,

As you see I'm sending on your Inc. Tax. Form. I've handed Pop your employment card as it has to be sent to the Labour Exchange. However I can't find your health card anywhere – did you let me have it, or have I let you have it back for something?

The place seems quite strange without you – and I'm sure Peter misses you terribly, he'll pine away soon! Barb is paddling along as usual, unruffled & as cheery as usual. Fifi[93] left us in the soup yesterday. Tuesday she asked if it would be OK to have Weds. Off – I said she'd better ask Pop, but I doubted as we are threshing. Well, the next we knew Fifi didn't come yesterday. When Mr Sque[94] came with the letters he was all "up the pole" about Fifi being the scapegoat while others had days off. However she turned up today – so far we are doing fine – Actually I think Bob must have been the cause of the trouble – Fifi would never have done a thing like that till she met him.

Anyway, we survived! I had my breakfast about 9 & fed some of the calves & eventually Mrs Spicer & I set off about 10.15. Barb did the customers by Curtis's and Careys Cottages as it was her short round & and we were back soon after one. Not bad going, I guess.

They've finished the threshing at the Kennels, & are now on the ricks near here, so I guess it'll be over this week.

That crazy vet Capt. Abbot made a lousy job of delivering Longman's calf & it bled from 12 noon till 8 at night – and then we only stopped it with boric acid & Vaseline – Joe's idea. I have to feed it out of a basin now so that it can't break open the wound against the side of a bucket. Joe & I are going to deliver the next one ourselves. I'll let you know what happens!

Your beloved Buster now has to be roped. After her calf was taken away yesterday, she played up like hec. & knocked the bucket against the wall, the stool half way down the shed & Joe managed to dodge her feet. Unfortunately I missed the sight, but she takes to the rope like a lamb – must have had some before.

Incidentally you've a week's wages to come. I suggested Pop made out a cheque, but he said that you'd come & get it. So I agreed, it's an excuse for you to come & see if we are still here. Of course if you ever feel the urge to milk a cow, we can supply you with the necessary four-legged animal – or as Andrew would say bovine quadruped!

I certainly hope Andrew can get out as he'd be very useful. He wrote to Pop saying that he was graded C3 U.K. only - & if only he'd registered as an "agricultural student" instead of just "student", or had unemployment cards, he could get out to work for the W.A.E.C.[95] or here. His C.O. advised him to try & get out but can't tell him how. If he doesn't get out he'll prolly end up as a nursing orderly. Poor Andrew!

Ah well, it's supper time so I am about to be shunted off the table. So cheerio, all the best & and I hope your cheery presence will aid your husband back to health.

Hope to see you soon,

Love,

Dot

A grazing pony in an autumnal New Forest

The Survival of the Diary

We were kneeling on the floor in the upstairs studio at Lanehead, sorting things before my aunt's move to Appleby-in-Westmorland. There were canvases, painting materials, boxes and papers all over the place.

My aunt reached over to a shelf and fished out two carbon copy soft-backed notebooks. "You must publish this after I'm gone. It's about my time on the farm in the New Forest." She was unusually firm.

After saying this she handed the books to me, then took them back and packed them up. I could see that they meant a lot to her, and could tell by the tone of her voice that I shouldn't ask any questions. She wanted me to discover the diary for myself and she was always a believer in "the perfect moment." She would have trusted that there would be the perfect moment for this diary.

Her request has turned into a wonderful gift. Preparing this diary for publication has taken me down many new paths and has brought me into contact with marvellous people. I've learnt so much. And I have a growing appreciation for the members of my family.

Through the work of family historian Dr. Diana Leitch, I've been able to discover more about my father's family – Aunt Anne was one of my father's sisters. I've learnt more about my grandfather and his side of the family which had grown away from ours. A cousin on his side of the family now has a photo on her wall of the cousins she never knew – my father and my three aunts.

It's been a privilege to learn about the Second World War and realise what huge sacrifices people made. These words have been said many times by many people, yet this has struck me beyond anything I can put into words.

I'll always remember my visit to the Special Operations Executive exhibit at the National Motor Museum, Beaulieu, to learn more about Uncle Marryat who had been an instructor there. The bravery of those secret agents is incredible.

Discovering the New Forest has been another wonderful thing. I can appreciate why the people who live there treasure their historic community where ponies, deer, donkeys, cows – and in the autumn, pigs – roam freely.

Tracing the land girls who were at New Park Farm at the same time as my aunt has brought me into contact with Freda Sque and her family. Now her daughter and I are regular correspondents. She's shared in the progress of the diary.

Inevitably the diary has re-connected me with my aunt, who was more of a friend and mother to me than an aunt. Always constructive and active, there was a lightness of spirit, joy, enthusiasm, humour, creativity about her. William Crawford, a friend of the family, described her perfectly when he wrote: "We all liked Anne, and indeed, who could not? She was so pretty, bright and intelligent; she never spoke without ensuring that her answer was wholly accurate and reflected precisely what she wanted to say."

There were many ideas which Aunt Anne followed in her life. One which I found particularly helpful was a Chinese saying which she took as a guide for living: "Know the things that make up your peace."

Of course, you will have discovered her already through the pages of this diary. And the diary is published just as she wrote it.

Shirley Nicholson
Manchester, 2011

A beast with magnificent horns roams freely in New Forest pasture

Biographical Details of Anne McEntegart 1905 – 1984

1905:   Born Anne Marguerite Patmore in Edinburgh, the youngest of four children.

1907:   The children's mother left their father and took them with her to Liverpool to live near her own parents, John and Julia Roxburgh. The children were brought up in Liverpool and had no further contact with their father. They never understood what had happened. It is now known that Anne's father remarried and became a successful businessman. Her mother, Annie Eliza, was a committed amateur artist.

Anne as child, seen here with her two older sisters, Marjorie and Vera, her brother, Robert, and her mother, Annie Eliza Patmore. Anne was the youngest in the family.

Anne McEntegart: *The Brae*, woodcut, 1920s
(Courtesy of Dumfries Museum.)

After 1918:   The family moved to The Brae, Crocketford, a few miles from Dumfries, and enjoyed an outdoor lifestyle.

Anne was involved with both the Brownies and Guides, and subsequently became Guide captain.

1919-1923:   Educated at Cheltenham Ladies' College. Made Head of House, summer 1923.

1920s: Took up advertising work with Crawford's Agency in London.

Illustrated two children's books written by her sister, Vera.

1925:   Began study of book illustration at The Edinburgh College of Art. Studies were cut short by mother who disapproved of a romantic relationship Anne was involved in at the time.

1926:   Sent abroad to live with sister Vera. Illustrations from a sketchbook from this period are used in this book.

1931:   Married Squadron Leader Bernard McEntegart at Fawley Parish Church, Hampshire. Husband, nicknamed "Mac", was stationed at nearby Calshot. Possibly Anne's first connections with the New Forest.

Anne was commissioned to make a series of advertisements for Fortnum and Mason.
(Credit: Fortnum & Mason PLC)

Anne McEntegart: *Amah's Head*, 1932. The head is of her son's amah, or nurse.

1931-1934:	Five days after their wedding, the couple left for Singapore. Mac joined No.205 Flying Boat Squadron on 17th January. His duties included a period of temporary command of the Squadron.
	Anne illustrated some English Readers for Malayan children as well as a Malayan cookbook. Also learned to sculpt, taught by Dora Gordine.
1932:	Birth of son, John Roxburgh McEntegart.
1934:	Family returned to England to live at The Pond House, Great Hampden, near Great Missenden. The house had been the country retreat of English poet John Masefield.
1939:	Second World War breaks out.
	Anne and John moved to Biggar, Lanarkshire, near her mother who was now living at Kirkwood, Coulter.
	Mac became aware of possible invasion and insisted that John should be evacuated to relatives in Newfoundland. Anne made the agonising decision to remain in England with her husband.
1940:	The couple occupied a house in Sloane Street, London. Anne was involved with "war work."
1943:	Mac was closely involved with preparations for the Dambuster Operation.
	Mac appointed Air Officer Commanding, Levant.
	Anne left London to take up work at New Park Farm in the New Forest. Although not an official member of the Women's Land Army, she did the same work as a land girl.
1945:	Closing stages of World War II.
	Anne left New Park Farm.
	Mac invalided out of the R.A.F.
	John returned from Newfoundland and the family lived in temporary accommodation until they bought Lanehead, a farmhouse with sixty acres of land, near the village of Dunscore, Dumfriesshire.

A photograph of Lanehead, taken from across the road.

1954:	Mac died.
1955:	Only son John died aged twenty-two, as the result of a training accident. He had followed his father in joining the R.A.F. and was a Flying Officer.
After 1955:	Moved to Paris to resume career as an artist and let Lanehead to a variety of tenants.
	Engaged in book illustration, made engravings and painted. Worked in oil, pastel and watercolour.
	Drove across the continent, travelling through Italy and Yugoslavia to Greece. From time to time Anne returned home to Lanehead.

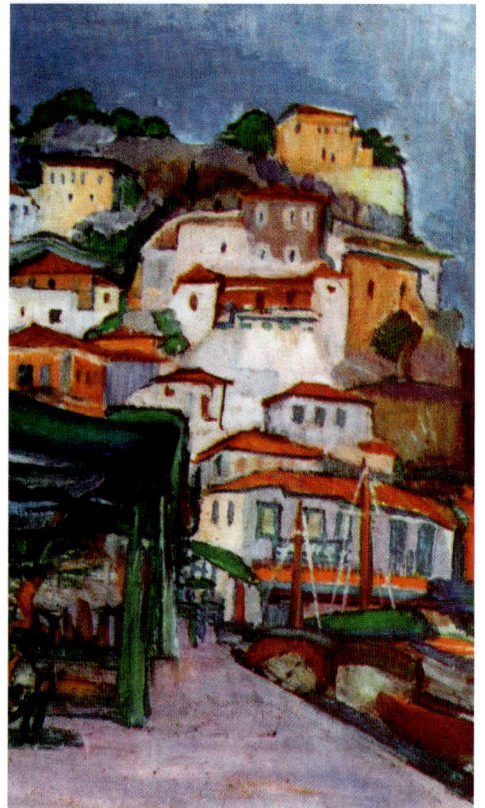

This is one of a series of Greek paintings which Anne was commissioned to do for greetings cards. This one is of the Greek island of Hydra.

The night before a solo exhibition of her work in Paris, the vehicle containing her paintings was stolen, along with all of her work. Anne never exhibited in public again.

1964-1965: Left Paris and returned to Lanehead.

Continued her work as an artist while travelling to many countries including Norway, Russia, Canada, Majorca and Iceland.

1979:

Anne at home at Lanehead with Hebe the springer spaniel, and Mr Thomas, the farm cat.

Moved from Lanehead to Georgian house in Appleby-in-Westmorland.

Becoming less mobile, Anne took up sculpting again.

1984: Died, aged seventy-nine.

1986: Retrospective Exhibition of her work at Abbot Hall Art Gallery, Kendal; The Gracefield Arts Centre, Dumfries; The McLaurin Art Gallery, Ayr.

This was organised by Jake and Shirley Nicholson. Anne had asked them to exhibit and sell her work after her passing.

Anne visiting Henry Moore's *King and Queen* at Glenkiln, with her devoted black labrador, Kelev. Glenkiln was not far from Lanehead and was a place she visited often. This sculpture was a work she particularly admired.

One of the New Forest's many picturesque roads. It's easy to imagine how Anne would have felt the serenity of her surroundings as she and Peter trotted along the milk round

Diary notes

1. To make it easier for the reader, the pronunciation of McEntegart is "Mac-En-Teg-Art."

2. New Park Farm was Anne's place of work from June 1943 to February or early March 1945. It had a long documented history going back 900 years. The farm was on land that had originally been a clearing for hunting deer. In the late 17th Century, Charles II granted a lease on the farm to (as an Echo Newsfeature put it in 1977) "one of the ladies of the court" for "services rendered." The farm buildings Anne knew had been built in 1853.

   While Anne was at New Park Farm, the tenant farmer was Walter Gossling whose family had farmed there since 1877. The farm's main concern was dairying, though to meet demands for more food production in WWII, Walter Gossling took to ploughing up new land for crops.

Walter, Kate and Dorothy Gossling at New Park Farm in 1924. By this point the Gossling family had farmed there for forty-eight years. Walter took over the tenancy of the farm in 1920.

After Walter's death in 1970, the farm tenancy was passed on to his only child Dorothy, and her husband Andrew Korbey. Dorothy had worked as a land girl alongside Anne at New Park. When her husband Andrew died in 1987, Dorothy continued to run the farm with her son John and his wife Caroline, until she retired at the age of seventy in 1992. John and Caroline ran the farm until 2004.

In its recent history, New Park Farm was taken over increasingly by non-farming activities including camping and polo, and is today no longer a working farm, but the showground for the New Forest Agricultural Show Society.

3. Freda was a local girl, the youngest child of postman, Jesse Sque. She had joined the Womens' Land Army some time in 1943, when she was seventeen. She left it in 1945, the same year she married a Canadian soldier, Bob Comber from the Queen's Own Rifles of Canada, who had taken part in the Normandy Landings.

    It was in the New Forest that a large number of Allied troops prepared for this great offensive against the Germans, as Anne was aware on her milk round. Bob Comber, later convalescing from his war injuries, was to write how impressed he had been when he first saw Freda: "When I saw this girl lift five gallons of milk about five feet up into a cooler, I thought, that's the girl for me!"

Freda Sque married Bob Comber, a Canadian soldier from the Queen's Own Rifles, on June 20th, 1945. From left to right are: Bob's uncle and aunt, Bob, Freda, Mary and Jesse Sque (Freda's parents). Olive Blachford is bridemaid.

4. So far we have not managed to find Eileen's surname, or where she came from. However, we do know that Eileen lived in a beach hut erected on New Park land. Roy, the young son of the farm's head cowman and his wife, Joe and Olga Fripp, remembers the hut vividly. One morning when he got up and looked out of the window of the cottage where the Fripps lived at New Park – New Park Cottages – the hut had vanished. He told his parents and they didn't believe him – until they looked themselves. The hut had indeed disappeared – into a deep hole in the ground. Some sort of Victorian drainage system had given way under it, though fortunately Eileen was away that night.

5. Whitley Ridge. In the 1995 book *Before We Go, Brockenhurst Memories of Peace and War*, the compiler Richard Taylor lists Whitley Ridge Hotel as one of the "large houses" in the area that was used for military purposes during WWII, in this case as "Officer's Quarters."

6. Joe Fripp was the head cowman at New Park Farm during Anne's time there. A big man with a very big appetite, Joe was definitely a character to be reckoned with; witty, tolerant but moody. One senses Anne liked him, and liked writing about him. Apart from his work on the farm, Joe made time to be "an avid gardener." He died in 1968.

7. Walter H. Gossling was Anne's boss. He was born in 1890 at New Park itself. Walter's father had become the tenant farmer there in 1877. After schooling in Salisbury, Walter planned to go into Estate Management and he trained with this aim in mind. It was during a two year practical course in forestry in the Forest of Dean that his father died. The eldest of four brothers, Walter was nineteen when he went home to New Park to manage the farm for his mother. He took over the tenancy in 1920. Because of a heart murmur, Walter had not been called up to fight in WWI. By the time of WWII he was exempted from joining up, as, like many other farmers, his work for the war effort was running his farm. A man of notable decency, tact and humour emerges from Anne's frequent mentions of Walter in her diary. He was elected a "Verderer" of the New Forest, and started his service in this unpaid but responsible job in 1956. The objective of the Verderers' Court was, and still is, to regulate and protect the interests of the commoners and to preserve the natural beauty and traditional character of the New Forest. John Korbey recalls that it was Walter's habit to walk round the entire farm each day. This meant he would have walked about ten miles by the end of the day!

A line drawing of Walter Gossling by the artist, Michael Ford.
This appeared in *The Hampshire Farmer,* Spring 1956. (Credit: N.F.U.)

8.	General Wladyslaw Sikorski, Prime Minister of Poland's London-based government in exile and Commander-in-Chief of her armed forces, was killed in a plane crash returning from a visit to Polish troops in the Middle East. He was sixty-two, and fifteen others perished with him, including his daughter.

9.	Thousands of Italian Prisoners of War were employed on the land in Britain. There were Italian POWs living near New Park, at Setley, a working labour camp half way between Brockenhurst and Lymington.

10.	Anne, a great book lover, is thinking of the disaster that ruins the honest, decent shepherd Gabriel Oak in Thomas Hardy's *Far From the Madding Crowd*. "A new sheepdog drives his flock over a cliff . . ."

11.	There are only two mentions of Vera in the diary. Vera was Anne's older sister, born in 1898. She went up to Newnham College, Cambridge and by the 1920s had begun research for a book on Daudet. This was published in 1949. In 1943 Vera was living in Brockenhurst which is more than likely the reason why Anne chose to come to New Park Farm. Vera left Brockenhurst on July 23, 1943. She had been living there to be near her husband who was with the Special Operations Executive, Beaulieu. Anne "sees her off to Edinburgh" on July 23, 1943, and initially felt that Brockenhurst was "empty" without her.
Her husband, Marryat Dobie - named after his great grandfather Frederick Marryat, author of *The Children of the New Forest* – was one of the first Training Instructors at Beaulieu. He was the longest serving instructor, also the oldest. However, a Confidential Report, 1942, said "... he possesses a puckish sense of humour and liveliness of mind which keeps him as young as the most junior instructors." In 1944 the National Library of Scotland applied for his release through the Treasury and the War Office accepted this.
A Confidential Report, 1944, noted "We say goodbye to him with the utmost regret." (see also obituary, The Times, November 2, 1973; The National Archives, P.R.O., HS9/437/1)

12.	Jack Phillips lived in the same row of cottages on the farm as the Fripps – New Park Cottages.

13	At the time of writing, nothing is known about "Joyce." Once or twice the diary hints that she may have been particularly friendly with Dorothy Gossling.

14.	Dorothy Gossling – Walter and Kate's only child.

15. There were two gypsy encampments at New Park. Most of the gypsies Gordon Philpott remembered from his childhood when he lived in the house adjoining New Park Farm had the surname "Whitcher". The farmers deliberately didn't pay them until the whole "season" was ended. John Korbey says he was told that the gypsies would celebrate "pay day" by lighting fires round their camps, regardless of the blackout, so the forest seemed to be ablaze. It was also remembered that the gypsies would fall out badly amongst themselves when drunk.

16. Roy Fripp.

17. From Rupert Brooke's poem *The Treasure* written in August, 1914. "...as a mother, who / Has watched her children all the rich day through, / Sits, quiet-handed, in the fading light, / When children sleep, ere night."

18. Gordon Philpott remembers Arthur. It was "Arthur Whitcher's lot" who fell out with "Fred Whitcher's lot" when they'd been drinking.

19. Sonny was Jack Phillips' son.

20. An untraced name – so far.

21. "John Bull's Daughters" was sometimes used as a name for land girls working patriotically in the fields. "John Bull" is a personified symbol of Great Britain, or particularly of England, much used at one time by political cartoonists. The phrase was the title of a popular song, composed in 1910.

22. This feeling for young people was something Anne never lost. She herself, from all accounts, "always retained a youthful spirit right to the last."

23. "The Park" was the name for some fields belonging to Walter, three or more miles away from New Park Farm. They were actually in Brockenhurst, near the level crossing and the cemetery.

24. This might be a slightly misremembered quotation, perhaps, from The Bible or *The English Prayer Book*. "The lines are fallen unto me in pleasant places..." *The Bible, King James' Version*.

25. Field Marshal Lord Wavell, Commander-in-Chief, and Viceroy of India.

26. The National Fire Service.

27. Air Raid Precautions. One might think of A.R.P. wardens peremptorily warning people who were not obeying the stringent blackout regulations after dark.

28. Roy Fripp remembers Carol Giblet, a little girl only a year older than he was, one of the three daughters of Jack Giblet. They lived in the same row of cowmen's cottages as the Fripps, but unusually, Jack didn't work on the farm. Roy recalls that he was a conscientious objector.

29. Anne is likely to be thinking of the painting by Jean-Francois Millet, the 19th century French artist who specialised in pictures of peasants. *The Angelus* was originally called *Prayer for the Potato Crop*. It is in the Musée d'Orsay, Paris.

30. Sarah was another member of the Whitcher family.

31. Most likely George was a member of the Whitcher family too!

32. The Canadians were a major part of the Normandy Landings.

33. A rare mention of Anne's son, still an evacuee in Newfoundland. In 1942 Anne had written a poem about this:

Overseas Evacuation

"Mummy where are you?" was the shout
Whenever Johnny was about.
He'd bang the door into the hall,
A moment's pause, and then the call,
"Mummy! Where are you?"

"I'm upstairs in the nursery!"
He'd bustle up, eyes bright with glee
To show me some peculiar stone,
To tell me all the things he'd done,
Then play beside me while I sewed,
At building bridges or a road.
But if perchance I left the room
I'd hear that call come very soon;
"Mummy! Where are you?"

I often wonder what he thinks
On hot days when he runs for drinks
Into that house so far away –
Does he remember NOT to say;
"Mummy! Where are you?"

34.   Farm pigs run free in the New Forest in the autumn, feeding on oak and beech mast. They also roam the Brockenhurst roads and lanes.

35.   St. Luke's Day is October 18. Luke was a native of Antioch who became a disciple of the Apostle, Paul.

36.   Mangel, sometimes called mangel-wurzel, is a vegetable with a plump root. Both the leaves and root are edible. More generally it has been used as animal fodder.

37.   Slightly misremembered quote from Thomas Hardy's short poem, *In Time of 'The Breaking of Nations'* written in 1915 during WWI.

38.   Anne means from New Park Farm to its milk round customers. A rare criticism of the management at the farm.

39.   It's not clear who Anne is quoting when describing her husband as an Air Commodore. Mac, born in 1891, had a distinguished career in the R.A.F., stretching from service as a Pilot in WWI to the end of WWII, by which time he had risen to the rank of Air Vice-Marshal.
       In 1928 he became personal assistant to Lord Trenchard, then Chief of the Air Staff. After Mac's marriage to Anne in 1931 he joined the No.205 (Flying Boat) Squadron in Singapore where his duties included temporary command of the Squadron.
       In 1932 their only child John was born. The family returned to England in 1934 where Mac took up a post on the Directorate of Research and Technical Development at the Air Ministry. In 1938 he took command of the Aeroplane and Armament Experimental Establishment at Martlesham Heath, Suffolk. Mac was promoted temporary Air Commodore on December 1st, 1940, by which time he was working as Chief Overseer at the Telecommunications Research Establishment.
       By the beginning of 1943 Mac had become Deputy Controller of the Research and Development Department of the Ministry of Aircraft Production. They were responsible for overseeing the development of the Dambuster bombs. It is believed among the family that Mac was one of those who helped persuade Churchill that the Dambuster Operation should go ahead. The night before the event on May 17th, 1943, he and Anne placed a bet that the operation would/wouldn't succeed. Mac had his concerns and was anxious for the men taking part. Anne won. The prize was a silver shilling which Anne wrapped in mauve tissue paper and kept until she died. Records show that Mac chaired meetings leading up to this event.

In 1943 Mac was appointed Air Officer Commanding, Levant. This was when Anne went to work at New Park Farm. In that post, according to the obituary in The Scotsman, September 29th, 1954, "... by his tactful handling of the delicate negotiations with the representative of the Vichy Government of France, he was able to save the ancient city of Damascus, the capital of Syria, from destruction by the bomber force under his command."

In December 1943 Mac was appointed temporary Air Vice-Marshal. In January 1944 he became Air Officer Administration, Headquarters Mediterranean Allied Air Forces. In 1942 he was made a C.B.E and in 1944 he was made a C.B. In 1945 the United States award him the Legion of Merit (Degree of Officer). The same year he was Mentioned in Dispatches.

(See obituary in The Times, September 28, 1954; obituary The Scotsman, September 29, 1954.)

Anne had written this sonnet to her husband in 1942:

To B.MC.E

I have had time to think of you today.
I saw your kind eyes patient through the years,
As with unquestioned faith you went your way
And never failed to comfort all my tears.
You set your course for both of us, as one,
Not blinded by the mists that dimmed my eyes
You looked beyond the clouds of doubt, and won
A vision of the sun each day arise,
And knew your path was set by one who cares
Not for the troubled heart, the anxious mind.
I too will banish all my empty fears,
And in this fleeting leisure I may find
That inner peace which only quiet can give,
Where silence in the heart alone can live.

40. For once a local gypsy whose surname was not Whitcher.

41. Very little has been found out to date about Olive. The "Olive" identified in the photograph of Freda Sque's wedding (see page 163) is Olive Blachford who was probably different from the Olive in the diary.

42. "Ley" is temporary grass. As *A Farm Dictionary*, 1953 puts it: "...especially grass meant to be ploughed up one year, or a few years, after sowing." The same book defines "ley farming" as "a farming system in which the fields in turn grow such crops as corn and roots, then are laid down to temporary grass for a few seasons."

43. Possibly rather exaggerated.

44. Anne's mother at this time was living in Castle Douglas. Anne would have walked round Carlingwark Loch.

45. The origin of this evident quotation has not yet been convincingly discovered.

46   The Countryman was, and still is, a long established monthly magazine focusing on rural issues.

47. Air Vice-Marshal.

48. A 'disc harrow' is an implement used for light cultivation and "is the kind that has sharp-edged saucer-shaped discs instead of tines. Also called disc cultivator." (Derek H. Chapman, *A Farm Dictionary*). A tine is one of the prongs of a cultivator, harrow, rake or fork.

49. Fordson tractors were built in Ireland and England after their production in the U.S stopped in 1928. Tractors were sometimes given nicknames such as "Lizzie" – perhaps because the work horses that had preceded them had names. Anne seems to have preferred a more formal address – Elizabeth and, later, Margaret Rose.

50. More properly, though not popularly, known as the DUKW, though pronounced DUCK: A six-wheel-drive amphibious truck originally designed by General Motors. The truck was used during WWII to transport goods and troops over both land and water, and especially for approaching and crossing beaches in such attacks as the Normandy Landings – D-Day. The initials were part of a General Motors naming system and stood for: D = kind of vehicle designed in 1942, U = utility, K = all-wheel drive, W = two powered rear axles.

51. Sago is a starch taken from the pith of sago palm stems used to make nutritious puddings. Its consistency was similar to that of tapioca. Sago was at one time (pre-1950s), also rather popular in the kitchens of English boarding schools. Anne may have encountered it at school or at home – or when she lived in Malaya.

52. In Richard Taylor's book *Before We Go, Brockenhurst Memories of Peace and War* there are a number of vivid recollections of the various bombs that fell on or near Brockenhurst. During Anne's time at New Park, in 1944, the area was subject to flying bombs.

53. One might suggest Anne thought of the tractors as princesses.

54. There are no recollections of Eddy.

55. Sunday of the Christian festival Pentecost, observed seven weeks after Easter each year.

56. Arthur C. Benson's book *The Thread of Gold* was published in 1905 – the year Anne was born. Although Benson was an academic, his writings appealed more to popular than academic readers. This book is reprinted today, but despite Benson's success when he was alive, he seems comparatively forgotten. In Anne's quite long quote, Benson is re-asking William Blake's question about the tiger: "Did He who made the lamb make thee?" That Anne felt strongly about this question is evident in the importance she gives to the Benson excerpt. Benson is remembered as the author of the words for the patriotic song *Land of Hope and Glory*.

57.   Like Anne, John Stewart Collis worked on the land during WWII. And like her he found ploughing, but in his case particularly with horses, to be fulfilling and profoundly happy work. It is no wonder she was attracted to the article by him that she mentions. (Much later – in 1973 – his book *The Worm Forgives the Plough* was published, becoming a classic of rural literature.) Working on the land in southern England during the war, both of them experienced a mix of old and new farming, of growing mechanisation hand in hand with traditional hard labour. Intriguingly, however, Anne the artist disagrees with Collis when he concludes that the straight furrow is the "labourer's acknowledgement of . . . art for art's sake." It seems that she saw a more practical side to ploughing straight furrows than Collis did.

58.   The Normandy Landings of June 6 1944, with American, Canadian and British troops launching a massive attack on the Germans in occupied France, was the "Second Front." The strategy was to comply with the wishes of Russia, one of the Allies, that the Germans should be attacked by an invasion of France. Stalin believed this would take the pressure off the "Eastern Front," where the Russians faced the Germans.

59.   "D-Day" was in fact postponed for one day because of the weather. This amphibious invasion of Normandy involved more than 160,000 troops. As the vast accumulation of troops descended on the New Forest preparing for D-Day, locals, including Anne on her milk round, were only too aware that that what was happening was massive. Roads were widened, troops and equipment were everywhere: Anne was very close to the build-up to this momentous event in the history of the war, and her description of its effects in the community she was part of, is particularly moving. Detailed information about this can be found in *Before We Go, Brockenhurst Memories of Peace and War* compiled by Richard Taylor, and *The New Forest at War* by John Leete.

60.   'Pilotless Planes' was an unusual term for the doodle bugs, but valid. It is likely that Anne had heard her husband talk about British experiments with pilotless planes.

61.   Anne quotes from Walter Rose's 1942 book, *Good Neighbours*. Rose made his name in 1937 when his book *The Village Carpenter* came out, which became a rural classic.

62.   Anne quotes the Harvest Thanksgiving Psalm from the *English Prayer Book* rendering of it.

63. From Shakespeare's play *Twelfth Night*:

    Viola: She never told her love,
    But let concealment, like a worm i' the bud,
    Feed on her damask cheek: she pined in thought,
    And with a green and yellow melancholy
    She sat like patience on a monument,
    Smiling at grief. Was not this love indeed?

64. Olga Fripp.

65. The O.O.A. is immediately remembered today by Roy Fripp, without any prompting!

66. Sarah Whitcher.

67. Barbara Carter, a local Brockenhurst girl, was born in 1925 and was still in her teens when she joined the Women's Land Army on the 10th of June, 1944. We know this because her daughter Denise recently discovered her mother's Women's Land Army release certificate, signed by the County Secretary on February 13, 1946. It shows Barbara's starting and ending dates of service. She married in 1948 and brought up her family in Brockenhurst. She had become very friendly with Anne on the farm. (see letter in the Further Word section, page 143)

68. Brownie was an old pony sometimes used by Anne when Peter was unavailable for the milk round.

69. Anne's education would have given her the kind of familiarity with the Bible that meant apt quotations from it would pop appropriately into her head, as in this instance. The occasion pointed up the difference between two sisters, Mary and Martha – between the contemplative and the over-busy. Jesus told Martha that "One thing is needful: and Mary hath chosen that good part, which shall not taken away from her." (*The Bible, King James' Version*, Luke 10, verse 42)

70. Anne certainly meant soldiers from the American South.

71. In WWI the Battle of Vimy Ridge on 9th April, 1917 saw the Canadian Corps sweep away German defenders who had been firmly entrenched there since September 1914. Vimy Ridge overlooked the Allied-held town of Arras and had therefore gained crucial importance in the war.

72. The original "Siegfried Line" was a line of defence in northern France in WWI. The English applied the same name to a German line of defence in WWII, built on Hitler's orders in the 1930's opposite the famously long French Maginot Line.

73. The flying bombs referred to earlier in the diary as Doodle Bugs.

74. In his 1932 book describing his experiences as the son of a farmer before and after WWI, the popular writer A.G. Street had what he called "an interlude" working in Canada. Eventually, thinking about returning home to England, he wrote: "Here I was a farm labourer, living a hard life with a complete absence of amusements and leisure..." For a number of reasons however, he decided to stay in Canada for a further year. One reason was that he "wanted to see the prairie, which I had broken, under crop... To go away and not see the first crop would have been the act of a traitor..." Clearly this sentiment had resonance for Anne.

75. Sir George Stapledon, author and lecturer, was an advocate of ley farming and an early apostle of the science of ecology. His books include *The Way of the Land* and *The Land: Now and Tomorrow*.

76. From A. G. Street's book *Farmer's Glory*. However, it seems that Anne must have confused it with the character "Mrs Lippett" whoever she was.

77. Presumably the "Agisters" charged with care of the forest. (see note 79)

78. "The Bench" is a popular New Forest landmark on the outskirts of Lyndhurst. It is a hill with fine views and is surrounded by grassy lawns, grazed by New Forest ponies. It is more fully named after the 18th century New Forest Keeper, the Duke of Bolton: "Bolton's Bench."

79. The New Forest Agister was originally "an officer of the king's Forest". From 1877 the Agisters became officials employed by the Verderers' Court of the New Forest. In 1932 there were two Agisters and in 1944 the number was doubled to four. The role of the Agister is to manage the commoners' stock on the Forest, carrying out instructions from the Verderers. In the spring they collect the "marking fee", which is the payment a commoner must make for each animal he wants to turn out on the Forest.

80. At the outset of the war the Minister of Agriculture and Fisheries appointed a War Agricultural Executive Committee for each county in England and Wales. They came to be known as "War Ags." Their main aim was to increase food production in their county.

81. North Weirs and South Weirs, which Anne mentions in the diary as exposed "high moorland", are two separate rough forest tracks. Both have houses on one side and forest land on the other. *The New Forest* by Elizabeth Godfrey and Ernest Haslehurst points out that one thing is certain: there are no weirs there, the only water being "ditch or bogland."

82. Anne is quoting from the fourth verse of a poem by George Meredith called *Earth and a Wedded Woman*:

    Rain! O the glad refresher of the grain!
    And welcome waterspouts of blessed rain!

83. Extracted from *Farmer's Glory* with a few minor inaccuracies.

84. Also known as "anti-radar tape" designed to disorient aircraft. It was made of silver and black foil, and much resembled videotape.

85. The "Western Front" was the most important fighting zone in WWI, and "no news from the Western Front" might, in WWII, symbolically signify lack of information about the progress of the war.

86. Presumably Brockenhurst's Morant Hall. (See page 18)

87. From Shakespeare's play *Love's Labours Lost*. School children were often required to learn this poem – one suspects, Anne included.

88. An echo of another poem Anne may well have learned; the ballad by John Keats, *La Belle Dame sans Merci*. The first verse reads:

    O what can ail thee, knight-at-arms,
    Alone and palely loitering
    The sedge is wither'd from the lake,
    And no birds sing.

89. A poem written by Anne in wartime London.

A London Room

I shall sit silent in my quiet room.
Grey walls outside encase me in a gloom,
Not sad, but still and silent, like some forest cool
Where thoughts can breathe, and peace enwrap my soul.
How soon from traffic's clattering noise and din
I can escape! And here in quietness win
A sense of silence far more strong, more still
Than found in country pastures, sunlit hill,
Where life must move and dare not stand,
Where light shines brightly on the land,
Where horses plough and men make hay,
Where countless noises fill the day.
Now wearied with the toil of war,
I find my rest within this door.
(1942)

90. A hotel since 1934.

91. Morant Hall, in Brockenhurst was a community centre built in 1911 for the whole area. The hall was demolished in 1971-1972.

92. Presumably there was more than one "Mrs Gulliver" in the vicinity who had her milk delivered. This one can hardly have been the same Mrs Gulliver described in Anne's diary who grumbled and caused so much trouble, finally switching to another dairy.

93. Freda Sque.

94. Freda's father, Jesse Sque, was a Brockenhurst postman who delivered the mail on a bicycle, but only as far as he could peddle.

95. War Agricultural Executive Committee.

Autumn in the New Forest

Acknowledgements

Grateful thanks to the family of Walter Gossling: John and Caroline Korbey and Steve Korbey, for their enthusiasm, interest and help.

Huge appreciation to Anne's family: Mary Doig and Alison Montgomery, with help from David Doig, Jean Gilliland, Anthony Montgomery, Sarah Montgomery, Simon Montgomery and Charles Patmore. Thanks are due to Grace Vera Dobie for her detailed account of Anne's maternal grandparents, John and Julia Roxburgh, written in 1981, and to Charles Patmore for notes made in 1982-3 on Robert Patmore's recollections of John Roxburgh.

Thanks to Anne's friends for their wonderful help - Guy and Maud Crawford, William and Marilyn Crawford, Cecilia Neal, Claire Petrenko and Susan Seright.

Special thanks to Freda (Sque) Comber for providing material for the book. Freda was a land girl at New Park Farm when Anne was there. Freda's daughter, Susan, has contributed photos, information and stories regarding the Women's Land Army at New Park Farm during WW11. Freda was born and raised in Brockenhurst. She was a war bride, living in Canada ever since marriage to Bob Comber. She thinks of her days in the W.L.A. with fondness and pride. Her ties to family, friends and the beauty of the New Forest are still very strong sixty-five years later.

Freda's nephew, Tony Johnson of Brockenhurst, has been a real friend of the book, generously sharing photographs from his own collection and answering many questions.

Thanks to Christopher Andreae for his work on the book. Thanks to Morven Andreae, Jayne I.Hanlin, Suzette Mitchell and Janet Ward for their vital help and support in this.

Much appreciation to Roy Fripp for his clear memories from his childhood at New Park. He has answered many questions.

Thanks too, to Gordon Philpott who was also a child at New Park , for his lively recollections. Grateful thanks to Denise Charlton, daughter of land girl Barbara (Carter) Street, for her enthusiastic help.

Thanks to Richard Reeves who has given unfailing help.

Much appreciation for the work of Victoria Keeves on two visits to the New Forest.

Richard Taylor, compiler and editor of the book *Before We Go, Brockenhurst Memories of Peace and War c1914 - 45*, has graciously given permission to use material from his book. Thank you.

Gratitude to Jane England who has helped crucially in the search for permission to use the illustrations of Evelyn Dunbar - wonderful illustrations to have in this book.

Grateful thanks to Patricia C. Byron for invaluable support and advice.

Robin Street of East Boldre has restored old photographs with the greatest care. Thank you. Thanks also for photographs from Mike Fear; the late Stan Orchard of Brockenhurst; Dumfries Museum; Anne Kramer; D.S. Colour Labs Ltd., Cheadle; Prudence Cumming Associates Ltd.; British Pathé Ltd.; the Estate of W.E. Sherwell-Cooper 2011 and the Amberley Archive; Christopher Andreae; Graham Cooper; Jo Holmes; Fred Phillips.

Gratitude to Marj Beattie for retyping the diary.

Appreciation also to Gill Clarke, Richard Cuzens, Dennis Dooley, Lynn Emery, Julie Jarman, Rita Legge, Dr. Diana Leitch, The Hon. Roger Montgomerie, Phil Morsman, R.W.O'Hara, Rosie Plunkett, Mavis Sacher, John Smith, Alice Strang, Kerry Watson.

Thanks to Peter Day for National Archives Research; Rachel Roberts, Archivist, Cheltenham Ladies' College; Susan Tomkins, Heritage Education Officer, The National Motor Museum, Beaulieu; Dr A. Tanner, Archivist, Fortnum and Mason plc; Dr. Philip W. Errington, John Masfield Society.

And appreciation to these institutions for their generous help: The British Library; Imperial War Museum, London; Imperial War Museum, Manchester; Lymington Public Library; Lymington Times; Lymington Museum; Ministry of Defence, Air Historical Branch (R.A.F.); Ministry of Defence, R.A.F. Cranwell; R.A.F. Hendon, R.A.F. Museum; R.A.F. Club, Piccadilly; Ministry of Defence Medal Office; The National Archives, Public Record Office, Kew; The National Motor Museum, Beaulieu; The Christopher Tower Reference Library, Lyndhurst Museum, New Forest Centre; Burns Monument Centre; Registrar's Office, Dumfries; The National Archives of Scotland; National Farmers' Union; Liverpool Record Office.

Last, but most importantly, thanks to the staff of RMC. Special thanks to Emma Robson for her real care for the book. Thanks to Paul Cocker for his co-operation and help. Gratitude to Martin Edwards for his committment to the diary.

This book is the result of the generosity, knowledge and kindness of many people. Thank you.

Bibliography and suggested further reading

Allen, Paul. Charles II granted farm lease for services rendered, The Echo, "Newsfeature" November 21, 1977

Antrobus, Stuart. "We wouldn't have missed it for the world," The Women's Land Army in Bedfordshire 1939 – 1950, Book Castle Publishing, 1st edn 2008, reprint 2010

Barnes, F.J, Powell, Orlando & Godfrey, Fred. John Bull's Daughters 1910

Benson, A.C. The Thread of Gold, 1st edn John Murray 1905. recent edn Wildside Press 2007

Brooke, Rupert. The Complete Poems of Rupert Brooke, Read Books 2006

Chapman, Derek H. (compiler), Dunbar, Evelyn (illustrator). A Farm Dictionary, published in association with The National Federation of Young Farmers' Clubs, Evans Brothers, Ltd. 1953

Clarke, Gill, Evelyn Dunbar, War and Country, Sansom and Company 1st edn 2006, reprint 2007

Clarke, Gill. The Women's Land Army, A Portrait, Sansom & Company 2008

Collis, Stewart, John. The Worm Forgives the Plough C. Knight 1973

Godfrey, Elizabeth (author), Hazlehurst, Ernest (illustrator). The New Forest, Blackie and Son Ltd 1912

Greenhill, Michael (author), Dunbar, Evelyn (illustrator) A Book of Farmcraft, Longmans, Green and Co. Ltd 1942

Grimwood, Irene. Land Girls at the Old Rectory, Old Pond Publishing 1st edn 2000, reprint 2005

Hall, Anne. Land Girl, Her Story of Six Years in the Women's Land Army, 1940-46, 1st edn Ex Libris Press 1993, reprint 1998

Hardy, Thomas. Far from the Madding Crowd, 1st edn 1874, recent edn Penguin Classics 2007

Hardy, Thomas. Thomas Hardy: The Complete Poems, Palgrave Macmillan 2001

Hodgson, Mary and Montiero, J.A. illustrated by Anne McEntegart, Our First Reader, from Nelson's New Readers for Malaya, Nelson 1930s

Joseph, Shirley. If their Mothers Only Knew. An Unofficial Account of Life in The Women's Land Army, Faber and Faber Ltd 1946

Keats, John. *Complete Poems of John Keats*, Wordsworth Editions Ltd 1994

Kenchington, F.E. *The Commoners' New Forest, An Outline of the Folk-History of the New Forest in the County of Southampton, its Peasant Pastoral Industry and its possibilities*, Hutchinson & Co (Publishers) Ltd 1st edn 1942

Kramer, Ann. *Land Girls and their Impact*, Remember When, an imprint of Pen & Sword Books Ltd. 1st edn 2008

Leete, John. *The New Forest at War*, The History Press, 1st edn 2004, reprint 2009

Marryat, Frederick. *The Children of the New Forest*, 1st edn 1847, recent edn Yesterday's Classics 2007

McEntegart, Anne. *1905-1984*, touring retrospective exhibition catalogue 1986

Meredith, George. *The Poems of George Meredith*, Phyllis B. Bartlett (editor), 2 vols., Yale University Press 1978

Moore, Henry. *Exhibition Catalogue*, Royal Academy of Arts, London, 1988

New Forest District Council, *The New Forest, its Character and Heritage* (a guide)

Nicholson, Mavis, *What Did You Do in the War, Mummy?* Chatto & Windus 1995

Patmore, Vera, *Six Introductory Reading Practice Books*, Thomas Nelson and Sons, Ltd. 1920's

Powell, Bob and Westacott, Nigel. *The Women's Land Army*, 1st edn The History Press 1997, reprint 2009

Rees, Josephine Duggan. *Corduroy Days*, Woodfield Publishing 2000

Rose, Walter. *Good Neighbours*, 1st edn 1942, recent edn Cambridge University Press 2010

Rose, Walter. *The Village Carpenter*, 1st edn 1937, recent edn Stobart Press Ltd. 1995

Searle, Adrian; Scott, Kitty; Grenier, Catherine. *Peter Doig*, Phaidon 2007

Shakespeare, William. *Love's Labours Lost* 1st edn 1598, recent edn Penguin 2000

Shakespeare, William. *Twelfth Night* 1st edn 1623, recent edn Filiquarian 2007

Shewell-Cooper, W.E. *Land Girl, A Manual for Volunteers in the Women's Land Army*, 1941, reprint by Amberley Publishing Plc 2011

Smith, Len. *Romany, Nevi-Wesh, An Informal History of the New Forest Gypsies*, Nova Foresta Publishing 2004

Snelling, Joan. A Land Girl's War, Old Pond Publishing, 1st edn 2004, reprint 2007

Stapledon, George. The Way of the Land, Faber and Faber Ltd. 1943

Street, A. G. Farmer's Glory, Faber and Faber Ltd 1933

Sweetman, John. The Dambusters Raid, Cassell, Ist edn Jane's Publishing Company 1982, recent reprint 2002

Taylor, Richard. Before We Go, Brockenhurst Memories of Peace and War c.1914-1945, MRM Associates Ltd., 1st edn 1995, reprint 1996

The Hampshire Farmer. Walter H. Gossling of Brockenhurst, spring 1956

The Hampshire Farmer. John Korbey of New Park Farm, date unknown, though after 1986

Tyrer, Nicola. They Fought in the Fields, The Women's Land Army, The History Press. 1st edn by Sinclair-Stevenson 1996, reprint 2010

Verderers of the New Forest. (five leaflets), Verderers of the New Forest; Agisters of the New Forest; Commoners of the New Forest; Pony Drifts in the New Forest; Stock of the New Forest

Verderers of the New Forest. The New Forest, Precious Wilderness or Suburban Park? The Verderers' policies for conserving the New Forest

Wyvill, Lynn. Nurturing the land, an army, and a family, newspaper interview, The Markdale Standard August 29 2001

The Scotsman. McEntegart, Bernard. Obituary September 29 1954

The Times. McEntegart, Bernard. Obituary September 28 1954

The Times. Dobie, Marryat. Obituary November 2, 1973

Country Ways, The New Forest DVD from The Country Ways Collection. www.countrywaysfilms.com

Dumfries Museum webpage on Anne McEntegart: www.artistsfootsteps.co.uk

Future Museum webpage on Anne McEntegart:

http://futuremuseum.co.uk/Collection.aspx/Anne_McEntegart

The ponies of the New Forest are free to roam where ever they choose

List of Illustrations

Index

Detailed map of the Brockenhurst area